THE GEORGE GUND FOUNDATION
IMPRINT IN AFRICAN AMERICAN STUDIES

The George Gund Foundation has endowed
this imprint to advance understanding of
the history, culture, and current issues
of African Americans.

*The Publisher gratefully acknowledges the generous support
of the African American Studies Endowment Fund
of the University of California Press Foundation, which was
established by a major gift from the George Gund Foundation.*

The Fifty-Year Rebellion

AMERICAN STUDIES NOW:
CRITICAL HISTORIES OF THE PRESENT

Edited by Lisa Duggan and Curtis Marez

Much of the most exciting contemporary work in American Studies refuses the distinction between politics and culture, focusing on historical cultures of power and protest on the one hand, or the political meanings and consequences of cultural practices, on the other. American Studies Now offers concise, accessible, authoritative, e-first books on significant political debates, personalities, and popular cultural phenomena quickly, while such teachable moments are at the forefront of public consciousness.

The Fifty-Year Rebellion

*How the U.S. Political Crisis
Began in Detroit*

Scott Kurashige

UNIVERSITY OF CALIFORNIA PRESS

University of California Press, one of the most distin-
guished university presses in the United States, enriches
lives around the world by advancing scholarship in the
humanities, social sciences, and natural sciences. Its
activities are supported by the UC Press Foundation and
by philanthropic contributions from individuals and
institutions. For more information, visit www.ucpress.edu.

University of California Press
Oakland, California

Library of Congress Cataloging-in-Publication Data

Names: Kurashige, Scott, author.
Title: The fifty-year rebellion : how the U.S. political
    crisis began in Detroit / Scott Kurashige.
Other titles: American studies now ; 2.
Description: Oakland, California : University of
    California Press, [2017] | Series: American Studies now
    ; 2 | Includes bibliographical references.
Identifiers: LCCN 2017005612 (print) | LCCN 2017008533
    (ebook) | ISBN 9780520294905 (cloth : alk. paper) |
    ISBN 9780520294912 (pbk. : alk. paper) |
    ISBN 9780520967861 (epub and ePDF)
Subjects: LCSH: Detroit (Mich.)—History—20th
    century. | Riots—Michigan—Detroit.
Classification: LCC F574.D457 K87 2017 (print) |
    LCC F574.D457 (ebook) | DDC 977.4/34043—dc23
LC record available at https://lccn.loc.gov/2017005612

Manufactured in the United States of America

25 24 23 22 21 20 19 18 17
10 9 8 7 6 5 4 3 2 1

A revolution that is based on the people exercising their creativity in the midst of devastation is one of the great historical contributions of humankind.

—Grace Lee Boggs

CONTENTS

OVERVIEW

INTRODUCTION

Detroit has stood at the center of a growing crisis in the United States tied to racial conflict, the collapse of the middle class, and political polarization.

Racism · Counter-Revolution ·
Polarization · Rebellion · Neoliberalism · "City of
Hope" · Election of 2016

CHAPTER I. 1967

While those who recognized the social causes of the "rebellion" advocated expansive social programs and investments to remedy racism and poverty, others stressed responding to the "riot" with repressive policing to restore law and order.

"Riot" versus "Rebellion" · Martin Luther King Jr. · Police
Brutality · Civil Rights · Black Power Movement · Kerner
Commission · STRESS

CHAPTER 2. THE RISE OF THE COUNTER-REVOLUTION

The hopes tied to Detroit's first black mayor faded as white flight and capital flight fostered a white conservative base of power in the suburbs alongside concentrated poverty and a housing crisis in the city.

Coleman A. Young · Suburbanization · White Flight · Reagan Democrats · Deindustrialization · Two-Tiered Society · Financialization · Wall Street · Foreclosure Crisis

CHAPTER 3. THE SYSTEM IS BANKRUPT

In 2003, Governor Rick Snyder ordered the state takeover of Detroit and installed an emergency manager with autocratic control over the city to enact a corporate restructuring plan.

Republican Party · Governor Rick Snyder · Emergency Management Law · Kevyn Orr · Public Sector Unions · Retirement Pensions · Municipal Bankruptcy · Privatization · Blight Removal

CHAPTER 4. RACE TO THE BOTTOM

The emergency management regime eliminated black "community control" and placed Detroit city government and the public school system in the hands of new leaders from the corporate class.

"Postracial" Discourse · Financial Consultants · Mayor Mike Duggan · "School Choice" · Betsy DeVos · Charter Schools · Closing of Detroit Public Schools · Catherine Ferguson Academy · Educational Achievement Authority

CHAPTER 5. GOVERNMENT FOR THE 1 PERCENT

With a trickle-down economic mentality enabling massive subsidies to corporations, Detroit's restructuring aided plans by two billionaires to control the city's central core, displacing low-income residents and small businesses.

Gentrification · Redevelopment of Downtown · Rebranding of "Midtown" · Mike Ilitch · Dan Gilbert · "Creative Class" · "Impact-Based" Development · Displacement of Low-Income and Disabled Residents · Demolition · Detroit Eviction Defense

CHAPTER 6. FROM REBELLION TO REVOLUTION

Led by African American women activists, Detroit's grassroots organizers have built movements that push beyond rebellion against an unjust system and toward a revolutionary reconstruction of society from the ground up. Detroit is an international model of resilience and creativity.

Women's Leadership · Water Shutoffs · "Freedom Schooling" · Environmental Justice · Urban Farming · Food Sovereignty · Black Lives Matter · "Peace Zones 4 Life" · Formerly Incarcerated Persons

CONCLUSION

The struggle in Detroit is pivotal to determining what type of political and economic system will emerge from the nation's current state of crisis and polarization.

"Shock Doctrine" · China · Automation · Climate Change · Karl Polanyi · The Great Transformation · "Butterfly Effect"

Introduction

What time is it on the clock of the world? What is humanity called to do at this moment in history?

Detroit's preeminent philosopher-activist Grace Lee Boggs is known for placing these profound questions at the forefront of every conversation. A veteran of the struggles for civil rights, black power, and social transformation, she sent a stern warning to the nation not long after her 98th birthday.

"With growing unemployment, the crisis in the Mideast, and the decline in this country's global dominance," Boggs declared, "we have come to the end of the American Dream. The situation reminds me of the 1930s when good Germans, demoralized by their defeat in World War I, unemployment and inflation, followed Hitler into the Holocaust."

"These days, in our country," she continued, "a growing number of white people feel that, as they are becoming the minority and a black man has been elected president, the country is no longer theirs. They are becoming increasingly desperate and dangerous."[1]

Her foreboding commentary was a pitch-perfect answer to Donald Trump's openly racist, misogynistic, and xenophobic appeals to "make America great again." Fed up with the "establishment," disgruntled, anxious voters in Michigan and the battleground Rust Belt states delivered Trump's decisive breakthrough. However, the event that prompted Boggs occurred well before 2016.

In 2013, the state's governor, Rick Snyder, stripped Detroit's elected government of its authority and named an emergency manager to take autocratic control over the entire city. The key elements that would later mark Trump's election facilitated the state takeover and bankruptcy of Detroit: authoritarian rule by the superwealthy; a "whitelash" against black political power; voter disenfranchisement; the gutting of workers' rights; and the pillaging of public goods and institutions.

The architects of this heavy-handed maneuver have put forward Detroit's corporate makeover as a precedent for financially distressed governments and public entities across the globe. From arts to zoos and from parks to pensions, every public asset, service, job, benefit, and regulation was put on the chopping block to be downsized, dismantled, or liquidated. Rampant home evictions, water shutoffs, school closures, and militarized policing disrupted life for thousands but became commonsense measures for ruling elites. Businesses were paid handsomely to plan, run, and redevelop the city. Detroit is the signature site where this antisocial gospel began normalizing ideas and practices that are pushing us toward a system of authoritarian plutocracy.

The sad reality is that the hazards millions of Americans fear in early 2017 most likely have already struck Detroit. The Great Recession that began for most of the nation in 2008 has been a multigenerational calamity for southeast Michigan. Once considered the wealthiest city in America, Detroit now has an official 40 percent poverty rate that is triple the national average. During the 1950s, Detroit's population peaked near 2 million. By 2015, it was estimated to be down to 677,116. According to the U.S. Census, the city is roughly 83 percent "black or African American," 8 percent "white," 7 percent "Hispanic or Latino," 1 percent "Asian," and less than 1 percent "American Indian and Alaska Native."[2]

These are symptoms of a systemic crisis. No city has come to embody the decline of middle-class economic security, the entrenchment of structural unemployment, and the burden of long-term debt more than Detroit. No region has come to embody racial divisions and the collapse of the political center more than metropolitan Detroit. To borrow from critical race theorists Lani Guinier and Gerald Torres, Detroit is America's canary in the coal mine. Too often it has been cast off as a space of exception—its problems so insurmountable that the nation refused to deal with them. However, Guinier and Torres call on us to recognize how embattled communities of color "signal problems with the way we have structured power and privilege" and "provide the early warning signs of poison in the social atmosphere."[3]

Speaking as a movement elder, Grace Lee Boggs was well positioned to sound that alarm. The daughter of Chinese immigrants, Boggs drew her wisdom from a lifetime of activism that began during the Great Depression amid financial distress, racial-ethnic scapegoating, and the existential threat of fascism. She had fought many of those same pernicious elements during six decades of organizing in Detroit, including 40 years partnering with James Boggs, her late husband and a black autoworker from Alabama.

The Boggses stood at the center of the movement in Motown. They saw union organizing integrate the shop floor and raise the standard of living for workers nationwide. They marched with Martin Luther King Jr., who first gave his "I Have a Dream" speech among tens of thousands of Detroiters of all races two months before the 1963 March on Washington. They watched African Americans become a new majority in the city and elect Detroit's first black mayor. Unquestionably, the most dramatic, impactful, and divisive event of this period was the 1967 Detroit Rebellion.

White fears, however, mirrored black hopes. With each new precedent and democratic advance, there arose negative forces acting to repel the prospects for transformative social change and restore old hierarchies. The Boggses called this reactionary movement the "counter-revolution." Detroit was targeted for disinvestment and political repression because it was a center of power for labor and civil rights. The toxic stew of economic dislocation and racial resentment made the region a breeding ground for all varieties of populism.

Grace Lee Boggs traced the origins of the counter-revolution to the aftermath of World War II. As African Americans migrated to Detroit and insisted they be treated as equals, white residents fled to the suburbs to preserve racial segregation and discriminatory control over local governance. "Taking with them their schools, their businesses and their taxes," Boggs commented, "they impoverished the cities and attracted the attention and money of extreme right-wingers like the Koch brothers."[4]

Detroiters have already borne the brunt of one-party rule over Michigan. With the Tea Party wave election of 2010, Republicans seized control of all three branches of state government. Governor Snyder had run for office as a political outsider drawing on his personal wealth and promising to use a businessman's acumen to shake up Lansing. Although self-identifying as a moderate, he presided over a dramatic shift to the right. Bipartisanship went out the door as the GOP gutted civil rights advances, passed antiunion laws, and hand delivered billions of dollars in subsidies and tax cuts to corporations. Because Republican leaders have recognized how unpopular some of these measures are, they have moved to preserve political power through gerrymandering and voter suppression.

With the right-wing U.S. turn coming on the heels of Brexit and an international surge in ultraconservative nationalism, a fateful through line connects the local, the national, and the global. The "post-racial" illusion has been shattered by a revival of white supremacy, unmitigated police killings, and the persistence of mass incarceration. As we teeter on the edge of ecological catastrophe and mass extinction, "free trade" has produced new extremes of wealth and poverty at the scale of city, nation, and world. Millennials and post-millennials fear they will be worse off than their parents, and the promise of never-ending progress and perpetual American superiority has evaporated.

A bevy of voices has sought to make sense of this indelibly fraught moment in history in which would-be signs of social progress—technological advancement, economic growth, and increased diversity—are producing new levels of economic and political polarization. Trump's election has drawn particular attention to books focused on white, rural, and working-class alienation and resentment ranging from the Deep South to the Upper Midwest. In notable cases, predominantly white communities have been ravaged by toxic environmental exposure and economic dislocation. Nevertheless, many voters in these areas harbor a libertarian repudiation of progressive proposals for state intervention and see people of color and immigrants, who are themselves experiencing adverse conditions, as threats and competitors. They frequently maintain a disdain for so-called secular liberal elites alongside the perception that urban nonwhite, immigrant, and queer populations are getting ahead of them through unfair advantages and government aid.[5]

These notable insights must be complemented by more investigations into the political terrain of urban America and communities of color.[6] New policies dubiously advanced under the banner of "populism" threaten to bring more pain to the multiracial working class. At the same time, activist forces—from the antiglobalization Battle of Seattle protest against the World Trade Organization in 1999 to Occupy Wall Street in 2011 and, especially, the ongoing Black Lives Matter movement—have been building momentum on the left. Challenging the complicity of Democrats with corporate rule, Bernie Sanders's upset win in the 2016 Michigan primary was a product and renewed catalyst of this momentum.

As millions of Americans fret over the next stage of polarization, I assert that paradigmatic developments in Detroit have both epitomized and shaped national trends. While I do not claim that the complex and multifaceted problems we face evolved solely from Detroit, I believe a case study of the city is essential for understanding our current crisis and the prospects for moving beyond it. My account is based significantly on independent research and observation through a decade-and-a-half of living and working in Detroit, but it is also a work of synthesis that would not be possible without the journalistic, academic, and activist sources cited herein.

Readers should be mindful of three overarching arguments that guide this book:

The counter-revolution is a reaction to a 50-year rebellion.

The overlapping political and economic crises confronting us today are a product of the neoliberal turn.

Despite the immense hardships and disparagement its peoples have endured, Detroit remains most significant as a city of hope and possibility.

REBELLION AND COUNTER-REVOLUTION

The definitive flash point for the rise of the counter-revolution was the Detroit Rebellion of 1967, which shook the nation to its core like no other. Detroit's uprising was part of a wave of urban disorders in which a predominantly young, black street force proclaimed its refusal to go along with a system that was too slow to accept racial equality and too quick to foreclose on the economic opportunities that had elevated tens of millions of whites into the middle class.

The rebellions of this tumultuous moment created a domestic crisis of governance and legitimacy that fused with international challenges to the U.S. empire from Vietnam and throughout the Third World. American leadership of the so-called Free World was rooted in the politics of liberalism as the centrist path between right-wing ideology, which accepted inequality as hereditary and fixed, and left-wing utopianism, which insisted that a revolutionary leap toward equality was desirable and achievable. Seeking to stabilize the industrial order, liberals acknowledged that capitalism was imperfect but appealed for mass support by promising incremental reform to build a future that was relatively more prosperous, inclusive, and egalitarian.

The crises of the late 1960s, however, provoked a polarized response, which we may see in hindsight as marking a point of no return. For an all-too-brief moment, policy makers saw the urban rebellions as a clarion call to rapidly accelerate the pace of liberal reform and racial integration through social investments and progressive reform on an unprecedented scale. Black Power activists went further, demanding "community control" of urban neighborhoods and institutions as an expression of self-determination and liberation. Hastening the rise of a black majority, Detroit's rebellion was followed up by the 1973 election of the city's first African American mayor, Coleman A. Young, marking the beginning of four decades of black leadership in city hall. Comparable to the sentiment of Americans hailing Barack Obama's election in 2008, Detroiters felt a new sense of hope and promise.

Counter-revolutionary forces, however, upended the political will for progressive or radical social change. Insisting that the urban disturbances be called "riots," they demanded heavily militarized policing and repressive criminal justice measures to restore "law and order." In this regard, the 1967 rebellion never really ended, as unresolved contradictions fueled a half-century of low-intensity warfare. Rejecting structural interpretations of urban and racial inequality, conservatives framed the crisis as a problem of urban pathology that merged stereotypes based on race, class, gender, and sexuality. The perpetual fear of "riots" cast black masculinity as a threat to "public safety"—an old trope dating back to slavery that took on new meaning with the disappearance of urban jobs. Stereotypes used to rationalize harsh labor discipline were repurposed to justify militarized policing and mass incarceration. Moreover, representations of the "absent" black father and the black single mother as "welfare queen" were further deployed to justify white flight to the suburbs as a defense of "family values."

Such narratives of black failure were mashed together by those condemning black political control of Detroit. For all the feelings of pride and accomplishment he evoked from his African American constituents, Young became the ubiquitous scapegoat for white suburban opponents to blame for urban decay. Making matters worse, the scale of Detroit's mounting economic woes surpassed anything Young and the newly ascendant black political class were prepared for. Among major U.S. metropolitan regions, Detroit developed the most extreme case of racial segregation and wealth disparity between a city and its suburbs. Mayor Young's counterparts were white suburban politicians like Oakland County's L. Brooks Patterson, who championed sprawl and balanced-budget conservatism while vetoing most efforts at regional cooperation. Patterson has been among the most prominent of voices reinforcing the narrative that whites lost Detroit and blacks ruined the city.

The 50-year tug-of-war began with black Detroiters gaining "community control," which was not entirely illusory but primarily a concession that would prove limited in scope and duration. The other end of the rope has been pulled by white nostalgia for a city that never was. Taken together, the state takeover, bankruptcy, and gentrification of the city can be seen to comprise a counter-revolution to "make Detroit great again."

THE NEOLIBERAL TURN

The crises of governance, legitimacy, and the family associated with the late 1960s era of rebellion were interconnected in a crucial manner with a crisis of profitability, creating what geographer Ruth Wilson Gilmore called "instability that characterized the end of the golden age of American capitalism."[7]

The response by capitalists to that crisis has been *neoliberalism*—
an umbrella term for the concerted effort of corporate interests
and conservative forces to push back the political challenge posed
by the movements of the 1960s and reverse the expansion of social
democratic policies and programs that defined the postwar era.
While class stratification and inequality are inherent properties
of the capitalist system driven by private ownership and profit,
neoliberalism has intensified these polarizing tendencies by undo-
ing measures designed to hold them somewhat in check. Through
the implementation of "business-friendly" domestic laws and
international "free trade" agreements, multinational capitalists
have achieved a dramatic rise in their power and flexibility over
the past five decades at the expense of the public commons and
the rights and remuneration of workers. The political and economic tsunami that struck Detroit in the era of deindustrialization was built on the neoliberal structures of intensified exclusion
and dispossession.

While the counter-revolution draws its energy from real and
perceived economic anxiety, it scapegoats non-elite social actors
for problems that are structural in nature. Twentieth-century
Michigan, and more specifically Detroit, was once the birthplace
of the American middle class. As the booming factories of the Big
Three automakers (GM, Ford, and Chrysler) drew scores of
migrants from the nation and the world, Detroit was simultaneously a marvel of advanced technology and the catalyst for the
modern American labor movement. The fall of the U.S. industrial order began with automation over a half-century ago and
was punctuated by the 2009 bankruptcies of GM and Chrysler.
In its stead arose a polarized world of cutthroat global competition resulting in spectacular wealth for the few and rising debt,
insecurity, and underemployment for the many. Although immi-

gration to Metro Detroit has been relatively low in comparison with other major metropolises, the sense that the region is on the losing end of globalization has fueled a nationalistic and xenophobic reaction that Trump's election dangerously stirred up again. As such, it is more critical than ever to understand the root causes of economic dislocation.

While the power of workers and unions has waned, new financial overlords have filled the vacuum. As business writer Rana Foroohar recently declared, "America's economic illness has a name: *financialization*. It's an academic term for the trend by which Wall Street and its methods have come to reign supreme in America, permeating not just the financial industry but also much of American business."[8] This perceptive insight must be extended to the public sector. Detroit's bankruptcy functioned as a hostile municipal takeover by financiers commissioned by the governor and emergency manager to reinvent Detroit on the basis of corporate restructuring principles. Their goal was to reinvest in revenue-generating sectors of the city by advancing gentrification, while ridding the balance sheet of the people and places deemed economic liabilities. What's more, the taxpayers were forced to compensate them at exorbitant hourly rates. This was an extreme version of the neoliberal restructuring taking place in cities, schools, hospitals, museums, and other formerly noncommercial entities nationwide.

Bolstering the ranks of billionaire cabinet members, Trump's selection of Michigan's Betsy DeVos for secretary of education signaled an intent to accelerate this trend at the federal level. The billionaire DeVos family has advanced a far-right agenda, spending millions to promote vouchers for parochial schools, for-profit charter schools, and policies that neutralize teachers' unions and public oversight. Drastic policy changes have sown chaos in Detroit and exacerbated racial inequality under the guise of "school choice." DeVos is one of many who entered Trump's cabinet advancing an Orwellian logic: Destroying public schools is the key to saving public education.

A CITY OF HOPE AND POSSIBILITY

Notwithstanding the advance of the counter-revolution and the pervasiveness of neoliberalism, I want to make clear that the current political crisis—at the level of city, nation, and world—is a sign of polarized choices rather than triumph or conquest. The long battle to define and shape Detroit's "revitalization" provides a window into the epochal conflict between two alternative futures, one characterized by the shift toward authoritarian plutocracy and the other by the commitment to participatory democracy. That is what is at stake for all of us living and organizing in the 21st century.

Perhaps more importantly than anything else, Detroit has attracted national and international attention as a site where hope, creativity, and opportunity have emerged amid intense crisis and devastation. Grace Lee Boggs was inspired to see an unprecedented coalition of organizations and people from diverse ideological backgrounds coming together to resist and defeat the growing counter-revolution. She further believed that while it was not easy, it was possible to build a movement that would address racial and economic anxiety, while inviting and challenging those with counter-revolutionary tendencies "to join with us in creating a new American Dream."[9]

Twenty-first-century Detroit reveals the transformative potential of organizing that is grassroots in character but responds to the array of global and local forces conspiring against the city.

Activists understand that oppression occurs at the intersection of race, class, gender, sexuality, geography, and ecology. Thus, they have worked to build intersectional movements that link together mobilization on multiple fronts and affirmations of difference across a multiplicity of identities. They see the forces of social change not as a unitary "mass" of bodies but more like a pluralistic collective of actors akin to what political theorists Michael Hardt and Antonio Negri have called the "multitude."[10]

The collapse of the factory system and its correspondent social order has led some of Detroit's most visionary organizers to go beyond conventional notions of redistributing wealth to reimagining the meaning of work and wealth. They strive to build a new model of postindustrial society based on noncommercial forms of local ownership and production rooted in cooperation and mutuality. This is evident, for instance, in movements for freedom schools, collective housing, urban farming, and community safety. In this way they have not only resisted forces of oppression, but have also sought to redefine and remake the social relationships that sustain life and community in the face of abject disposability and a crisis of sustainability.

During my time in the city, Detroit came to represent the pertinent reminder of unfulfilled hopes and the idealistic promise of unfinished agendas in the Obama era. Now, as a darker, cynical mood has set on the nation and world, the struggles of Detroiters to survive under conditions of extreme adversity while creating mental and physical space to imagine radical alternatives may prove more illuminating than ever.

ONE

1967

America changed forever in 1967.

For the purposes of our story, the year began on April 4, the day Martin Luther King Jr. broke his silence over the Vietnam War. Condemning U.S. military intervention in Southeast Asia, he declared that "the nation must undergo a radical revolution of values" to conquer "the giant triplets of racism, extreme materialism, and militarism."[1]

Exactly one year later, Dr. King and his dream of an integrated nation guided by justice were gunned down at the Lorraine Motel in Memphis, Tennessee.

In the middle of that tumultuous and eventful year, the eyes of Dr. King, as well as those of the entire nation and much of the world, were focused on Detroit. On July 23, 1967, the struggle over alternative futures took a dramatic turn when the city erupted in a rebellion that raged over four days of liberation and destruction, of hope and peril. Detroit was central to an overall pattern of social rebellion in 1967–68. The historical moment was further marked by the mass revolt against American imperialism in Vietnam and sites throughout the Third World, dozens of small and large outbreaks of urban rebellions across the United States, and radical and militant forms of organizing and movement building among and between communities of color, indigenous peoples, feminists, queer communities, disabled persons, workers, and environmentalists.

Explaining his antiwar stance, King proclaimed: "I knew that I could never again raise my voice against the violence of the oppressed in the ghettos without having first spoken clearly to the greatest purveyor of violence in the world today—my own government." His moral outrage at foreign wars was paralleled by a domestic concern "that large segments of white society are more concerned about tranquility and the status quo than about justice and humanity." Recognizing that "a riot is the language of the unheard," King stressed the need to condemn the "intolerant conditions" that left many with "no other alternative than to engage in violent rebellions to get attention."[2]

Detroit epitomized this general rebellion of 1967 that upended the old social order but fell short of instituting a new one. In the eyes of James and Grace Lee Boggs, the movements opened up more contradictions than they resolved. Despite the twists and turns from five decades of rebellions and reform, of counter-revolution and repression, an underlying fact remains: the social tensions and conflicts we are grappling with today can be traced directly and indirectly to the divisions that tore apart the nation in 1967.

THE ROOTS OF REBELLION

It is an understatement to say Detroit has never been the same since the great rebellion. Indeed, people under the age of 50 only know Detroit by what it became after 1967, a proud black-majority city beset by economic hardship, scorned by its suburban neighbors, and mocked or forgotten by the rest of the nation.

Those who look back at Detroit before 1967, especially the city's white former residents and their descendants, often do so primarily through the lens of nostalgia. They recall arriving in town at the grand Michigan Central Station, spending the holiday season at the downtown Hudson's department store, and cheering the home team at old Tiger Stadium. Detroit was the "Paris of the Midwest" in its golden age, but most of the glittery symbols of that era have been abandoned or demolished. Beyond the spectacle, Detroit was known as a city of industry—or, more specifically, a city of work. It was a site of opportunity and reward for those who put in their time. The nostalgia for pre-1967 Detroit is ultimately rooted in the day-to-day existence of working-class and middle-class families who lived in single-family homes within vibrant neighborhoods filled with well-functioning schools, churches, and business strips.

Conveying a mix of sadness, tragedy, anger, and regret, these nostalgic images provide a deep sense of what white America felt it lost in the Detroit Rebellion of 1967. This deep sense of loss, in turn, informs what these ex-Detroiters would like to bring back or take back. In this way, today's impulse to "make America great again" echoes the discourse defining Detroit for the past half-century.

Nostalgia for the city's so-called golden age before 1967, however, overlooks a plethora of inconvenient truths about pervasive and longstanding patterns of racism, discrimination, and police brutality in Detroit and America. Detroit had a storied place in history as a stop on the Underground Railroad, but its settlement was defined by the seizure of indigenous lands and antiblack racism. Industrial-era Detroit drew thousands of African Americans fleeing the Jim Crow South as part of the Great Migration. During the 1920s, however, the city's Ku Klux Klan chapter had over 20,000 members, many of whom took root within the Detroit Police Department. The average white citizen did not need to be a Klan-sympathizer to share its goal of confining African Americans to substandard, segregated housing.[3]

Giving rise to the modern American labor movement, the struggles of Detroit and Michigan factory workers during the Great Depression and World War II set a new national standard for livable wages and job security backed by union contracts. Propelled by the heroic sit-down strikes against Detroit's major car companies, the United Auto Workers became an economic and political force that embraced civil rights measures. Black workers, nonetheless, generally remained stuck in the lowest-paid, "meanest and dirtiest" jobs. When Detroit's massive factories became the "arsenal of democracy" against fascism, the federal government enacted historically unprecedented fair-employment policies to promote maximum participation in the workforce. In response, thousands of white workers went on "hate strikes" to protest the notion of working alongside even a handful of African American workers in integrated workplaces. Racial tensions in the city exploded in June 1943 in a disorder properly called a "race riot"—a term that, prior to the 1960s, almost always referred to white mob attacks on the black community. Of the 34 who died in the 1943 riot, 25 were African American, most of them killed by the police.[4]

While Detroit became a hotbed of movement building during the postwar era, civil rights activism brought slow and incremental progress in the long march to freedom. The first black city council member in Detroit's history did not take office until the 1950s. During the '60s, new progressive policies were implemented under Jerome Cavanagh, the young mayor who upset the conservative establishment and carried the aura of John F. Kennedy's Camelot. Two months before the national 1963 March on Washington, Martin Luther King Jr. locked arms with the city's civil rights leaders and 200,000 Detroiters in the Walk for Freedom. Backed by an interracial coalition, Cavanagh drew tens of millions of dollars in federal funding to promote jobs, education, health care, child care, and other measures aimed at creating what President Lyndon B. Johnson called the Great Society. Moreover, Detroit served as the exemplar for the federal Model Cities program, which was an urban pillar of the War on Poverty.[5]

In hindsight, Cavanagh's reforms were woefully inadequate, but they helped relieve unemployment and moved further in the direction of racial equality than the agendas of any of his predecessors. Part of the problem stemmed from implacable white opposition. In 1963, for instance, Detroit's city council voted overwhelmingly to reject an open-housing ordinance and even passed a resolution affirming the right of white homeowners to refuse to sell to black buyers. White denial comprised another aspect of the problem. Two scholars reported that Wayne State University fired them and terminated their urban studies program for drawing attention to the persistence and worsening of racial segregation and discrimination in Detroit.[6]

Police brutality and racism within the criminal justice system consistently undermined black hopes for dignity and fair treatment. Despite Cavanagh's steps toward integration, the Detroit Police Department remained less than 3 percent black through the 1950s and reached only 5 percent by 1967. The force was both overwhelmingly white and noxiously racist. Cavanagh's first police commissioner reported that 90 percent of the city's cops were "bigoted." They subjected African Americans to humiliating and unconstitutional stop-and-frisk searches and routinely beat suspects to enact justice through the "alley court." Corruption was rampant within the ranks and led to shakedowns that particularly heightened the abuse of black women sex workers. The most notorious cops belonged to units referred to as the "Big Four," featuring a driver in uniform accompanied by three plainclothes officers to surround, harass, and brutalize black civilians.[7]

Whites lived in an alternate reality from African Americans—when the subject of race was broached in general, but especially when the focus was on policing. Reports of black criminality and violence led to blanket racial stereotypes degrading the African American community while sanctifying white guardians. Roughly 80 percent of whites in Detroit considered the police to be fair and unbiased. Indeed, Detroit's men in uniform saw themselves as the real victims, regularly claiming that the shooting or beating of African Americans was justified by self-defense or suspects resisting arrest. As city leaders refused the consistent demand for a civilian review board, police misconduct was rewarded and reinforced by racism and corruption among prosecutors and judges.[8]

By ignoring these historical realities, the nostalgic story of Detroit facilely blames the city's downfall on the 1967 "riot"—cast as one and the same moment with the rise of the Black Power movement and the 1973 election of Coleman A. Young. The profound social divisions that have shaped and scarred southeast Michigan over the past half-century are in many ways encapsulated in the riot-versus-rebellion debate. From the events of the 1960s to the recent protests against police killings in Ferguson and Baltimore, the use of the term *riot* focuses attention on acts of violence or lawlessness. The hard racist or authoritarian sees rioters as animals that need to be put down or caged. These racial stereotypes intersect with sexual stereotypes, pervasive during slavery and Jim Crow, of black men as sexual aggressors seeking to prey on white women. The relatively moderate perspective, while acknowledging that legitimate social problems may need to be addressed, emphasizes that a riot solves nothing or makes the situation even worse. Hence, the immediate concern remains policing the "riot" and restoring order.

In contrast, to use the term *rebellion* is to foreground the intrinsically political nature of the disturbance. As Grace Lee Boggs stated, "We in Detroit called it the rebellion [because] there was a righteousness about the young people rising up." Those who took to the streets were standing up "against both the police, which they considered an occupation army, and against what they sensed had become their expendability because of high-tech."[9] As white elites and multinational corporations found ready substitutes for black labor, black bodies once viewed as competition for jobs came to represent a problem to be ignored, contained, and eliminated.

THE REBELLION AND THE POLICE RIOT

In the early morning of July 23, 1967, the Detroit police raided an after-hours club in the city's 12th Street neighborhood on the near northwest side of town. Although this type of venue—known as a "blind pig" and selling booze outside of the hours of regulation—was not strictly legal to operate, it was not uncommon either. Many of such kind had existed within the city since the days of Prohibition. The police, however, had targeted this one with fervor, attempting to raid it nine times within the past year. The owner of the blind pig insisted that the July 23 raid was a shakedown. When the police moved to arrest everyone in the bar—85 African American patrons—crowds outside became incensed as they witnessed acts of police brutality (but none the police would admit to). This incident touched off four days of rebellion that involved 43 deaths and over 7,000 arrests, nearly double the number arrested in the 1965 Watts Rebellion.[10]

Historian Sidney Fine authored an extensive account of the "Detroit Riot of 1967" in *Violence in the Model City*. For tens of thousands of whites in the city, the rebellion represented their worst nightmares come to life. It should be pointed out that some whites sympathized with the politics of rebellion, quite a number participated in looting, and 12 percent of the arrestees were white. For the most part, however, white Detroiters saw a breakdown of law and order—and hostility directed at them by African Americans. Dismissing any political definition of the disturbance, the *Detroit Free Press* in its 10-year retrospective characterized it as "a meaningless event that stimulated nothing, contributed nothing, revealed nothing of any substance or durability."[11]

While black Detroiters who were surveyed initially described the event as a "riot," the majority, by a wide margin, gravitated to calling it a "rebellion." They viewed it as an expression of black unity and a political declaration for their "fair share" of resources and power in the city and the nation. Activist Ed Vaughn described the "strong sense of camaraderie" that black Detroiters "enjoyed" after the rebellion. "We felt that we had accomplished something," he recalled, "that the riots had paid off, that we finally had gotten the White community to listen to the gripes and to listen to some of the concerns that we … had been expressing for many years."[12]

Regardless of opinion, when we look closely at the deadly violence that took place during the rebellion, one pattern stands out: the killing of African Americans by state actors. Of the 43 who died, 33 were black and 30 were killed by law enforcement, as the streets of Detroit were covered by 17,000 Detroit cops, state police, National Guardsmen, and finally U.S. Army troops. Authorities had hoped initial outbreaks of violence would play themselves out. When they instead expanded into full-fledged rebellion, the police became the aggressors in one confrontation after another. "This is more than a riot," said one police officer, reflecting the view of many peers. "This is war."[13]

When Governor George Romney called in the National Guard, they were poorly prepared and rushed into action. Many had signed up to avoid being sent to Vietnam, yet they also had little prior experience in or knowledge of Detroit when they were deployed to the city. "I'm gonna shoot anything that moves and that is black," one declared. In one of the most horrific episodes, a four-year-old African American girl named Tonia Blanding was struck 27 times after the National Guard mistook the lighting of a cigarette for sniper fire and saturated her apartment building with .50 caliber machine gun fire. When the final count of the dead was tallied, most had been killed by the police and guard. The army, under direct orders, exercised comparative restraint and carried unloaded weapons.[14]

From the vantage point of thousands of black Detroiters, the civil disorder was experienced largely as a violent police riot, recreating what had occurred in 1943. Whatever resentment the black street force may have felt toward "whitey," the rage was almost uniformly directed at property rather than human life. Nonetheless, the police systematically rounded up, illegally searched, beat, and arrested scores of black Detroiters, including members of the press and citizens doing nothing more than observing events. Hundreds of suspects were detained in poor and unsanitary conditions; most notoriously, up to a thousand were forced to sleep, urinate, and defecate on a cement floor of the police department's underground parking garage. Many were subsequently railroaded by an overstressed legal system with little regard for due process. Misogyny underlay abuse, as well. One woman was falsely arrested and then groped, molested, and forced to strip for a photograph with an officer fondling her half-naked body.[15]

The most widely publicized travesty of justice occurred at the Algiers Motel on Woodward Avenue. Three young black men aged 17 to 19—Carl Cooper, Aubrey Pollard, and Fred Temple—were killed by the police, while seven others were detained for hours, interrogated, and tortured. Investigations determined that the cops were never fired on. What set them off was finding two white women in the company of black men; their visceral revulsion at the apparent sexual transgression seemingly extended their imperative to restore order from the public streets to the private bedroom. Policing the riot thus translated into preserving white patriarchy through egregious brutality to keep black masculinity and white womanhood in their proper places. Cooper, Pollard, and Temple were shot in a manner consistent with execution. After giving evasive and contradictory accounts, three officers, Ronald August, Robert Paille, and David Senak, eventually admitted to the shootings and were forced to stand trial. The court proceedings, however, proved to be loaded in favor of the police. One trial had a change of venue to Mason, Michigan, a small town that was 99 percent white. A federal conspiracy trial was sent to Flint, where all the black potential jurors were removed on the charge that they were inherently biased. In every case, the officers were found not guilty.[16]

"THERE IS NO SUCH THING AS
MODERATE ANY MORE"

While the flames were still burning in Detroit on July 27, 1967, President Johnson announced the formation of the National Advisory Commission on Civil Disorders. Chaired by the governor of Illinois, Otto Kerner, it has since become known as the Kerner Commission. The "basic conclusion" of its March 1968 report has been quoted endlessly: "Our nation is moving toward two societies, one black, one white—separate and unequal." While the commission examined 164 urban disturbances from the first nine months of 1967, Detroit was its major concern. Because its membership consisted primarily of white elites hand-picked by the president, its diagnosis and prescription caught many off guard. More than ready to assign blame, it bluntly declared that "white racism is essentially responsible for the explosive mixture which has been accumulating in our cities since the end of World War II." The commission warned of "the continuing polarization of the American community and, ultimately, the destruction of basic democratic values." It called for unprecedented attention to the structural conditions of racism, discrimination, and inequality.[17]

The Kerner Commission documented job discrimination and housing segregation while drawing attention to police brutality and the "double standard" of justice that led many blacks to see the cops as symbols of "white power, white racism and white repression." These systemic forms of racism had created a "state of crisis" for African Americans in cities like Detroit. In response, it called for a deep commitment to social programs that would "require unprecedented levels of funding and performance." It identified an immediate need for 2 million new jobs—no fewer than 1 million in the public sector—to jump-start this process. And it explicitly called for taxes to be raised to fund these programs, concluding "There can be no higher priority for national action and no higher claim on the nation's conscience."[18]

Conservative critics, however, faulted the commission, the president, and liberals in government for weakening the nation by being soft on crime. When the Kerner Commission's report was published, the Republican candidate, Richard Nixon, was on his way to winning the presidency by promising to restore "law and order" for the "silent majority" chafing at the state of rebellion in America. Nixon condemned the commission for blaming "everybody for the riots except the perpetrators of the riots." What the rebellions signaled for Nixon and his followers was the need for a steeled man in the White House with the resolve to "meet force with force, if necessary, in the cities." During his final year in office, President Johnson was scarcely more supportive of the commission's report than his GOP rival. As historian Julian Zelizer recounts, LBJ cast it aside and declared its recommendations to be politically impracticable. Johnson's repudiation of his own commission went so far that he stopped discussing it with the media.[19]

In the aftermath of the rebellion, black radicals of varying tendencies escalated their presence in Detroit. As Francis Kornegay of the Detroit Urban League surmised in August 1967, "There is no such thing as moderate any more—only militant and more militant." For founding members Ron Scott and Eric Bell, the Detroit chapter of the Black Panther Party was built from a desire to harness the energy of the rebellion into concrete organization. The Detroit chapter organized the national party's signature survival programs, such as free breakfast for children, and later a wing committed to armed resistance. While the Panthers turned heads among the people and the police, they were one of many groupings seeking to seize the time. Situating black workers at the vanguard of a movement to overthrow capitalism, the Dodge Revolutionary Union Movement, commonly known as DRUM, built on Marxist notions of struggle to organize wildcat strikes that intensified the spirit of rebellion within the factories of the Motor City. As new branches of the Revolutionary Union Movement spread to other plants and sites, its leaders left no doubt that they would challenge not only the auto companies but also the United Auto Workers, charging that the union was complicit in a system of race and class oppression.[20]

In a feature for the *Detroit News,* Louis Lomax, a nationally prominent African American journalist, named six people whom the city's black establishment deemed most responsible for fanning the flames of rebellion. The six identified, who had worked together on projects like the Freedom Now Party's all-black slate for the 1964 election, were Reverend Albert Cleage, Milton and Richard Henry, James and Grace Lee Boggs, and Ed Vaughn.[21] It was an irresponsible and grossly inaccurate attempt to cast aspersions of blame for the violence on figures well known within the Black Power movement. Yet Lomax did manage to identify radicals whose subsequent political trajectories exemplified some of the key directions of Black Power militancy after 1967. Cleage, who later changed his name to Jaramogi Abebe Agyeman, founded the Shrine of the Black Madonna and developed a large and loyal following for what he called Black Christian Nationalism. The Henry brothers organized the Republic of New Africa (RNA) and determined to build an independent black nation in the South. While the RNA pledged to liberate five southern states under white rule, the Boggses declared that "the city is the black man's land." In 1969, James Boggs issued a "Manifesto for a Black Revolutionary Party" based on principles of Marxist-Leninist vanguardism, though over time the Boggses moved toward multiracial visions of revitalizing the postindustrial city from the ground up. Of the six named, Vaughn, whose bookstore was a hub of Black Power ideas and meetings, moved most decidedly into the electoral arena.[22]

While the rebellions fired up the imaginations of those looking to topple the system, the presence of radicals was magnified by agents of the state seeking to justify repressive measures. Harboring fears of black "terrorists" and insurrection, white residents commonly responded to the rebellion by expressing a desire for more policing and protection. The Detroit Police Department triggered a major confrontation with the RNA when it moved to break up an event the organization held at the New Bethel Church on March 29, 1969. One police officer was killed, and 142 RNA members were rounded up and arrested. Those staunchly committed to nonviolence were not spared similar police assaults. On May 13, 1968, demonstrators carrying forward MLK's plans for the Poor People's Campaign—men, women, and children alike—were trampled by 15 to 20 mounted cops. Under J. Edgar Hoover, the FBI's Counterintelligence Program (COINTELPRO) developed systematic plans and unconstitutional tactics to conduct surveillance on activists and to disrupt both peaceful and militant protest movements throughout the nation. No target was a higher priority for the FBI than the Black Panthers. "From the very beginning, police were harassing us, sending in infiltrators," remembered Ron Scott. "They had fresh memories of '67 and did not want to see rebellion institutionalized."[23]

As political advocates of "law and order" deliberately blurred the line between war and rebellion, they called for the militarization of local law enforcement. In the immediate aftermath of the rebellion, the Detroit Police Department requested $2 million in new equipment, including armored personnel carriers, automatic rifles, and thousands of grenades. Within a few months of the rebellion, 300 Detroit cops had joined the National Rifle Association because it afforded access to military surplus weaponry. Gun sales in the city skyrocketed among civilians as well.[24]

The 1969 mayoral election proved to be gut-check time for both the radicals and the more mainstream civil rights leadership in Detroit. Nixon's national call for "law and order" was taken up by the sheriff of Wayne County, Roman Gribbs, who edged out Richard Austin, the first black candidate to win a mayoral primary in the city's history. (It was a near carbon copy of the election held earlier that year in Los Angeles, where Sam Yorty defeated a moderate, black city council member, Tom Bradley, by playing on smoldering white fears of rebellion.) As mayor, Gribbs carried through on his signature agenda by launching a policing campaign called STRESS: Stop the Robberies, Enjoy Safe Streets. Formed in January 1971, STRESS holds a place of true infamy in Detroit lore. Ostensibly, its goal was to clean the streets of criminal elements by luring them to attack undercover officers posing as decoys. In practice, this often meant the police had carte blanche to brutalize and murder those they deemed suspects. Within nine months of operation, STRESS officers had killed 10 suspects, all but one of whom were black. Two years later, the number killed reached 22. STRESS accounted for only 2 percent of the police force but one-third of all police killings. Detroit claimed the dubious distinction of leading the nation in civilians killed by the police.[25]

Few involved in Detroit's post-rebellion governance seemed ready to heed the Kerner Commission's warnings of the "grave danger" of "overreaction" and the "incalculable" damage that would be caused by police arming themselves with "mass destruction weapons [that had] no place in densely populated urban communities." As historian Elizabeth Hinton has pointed out, STRESS was a signature move in the national paradigm shift from the War on Poverty to the War on Crime, driven by a heightened focus on surveillance and arrest in response to public fears of "urban guerilla warfare."[26] STRESS had the exact impact its bombastic acronym suggested it would. Rather than settle matters or solve problems, it aggravated social tensions and divisions to the breaking point. It was part and parcel of a rightward policy shift that widened the fault lines that had been sharply carved into the metropolitan landscape along the axes of race, class, and geography.

Though the fires were extinguished and the violence quelled, the rebellion never truly ended—not for the suburbanites, who still feel they are under siege and must continually act to repress an ongoing threat of insurrection; and certainly not for the urban neighborhoods of Detroit that are still grappling with the underlying problems that sparked the rebellion, while being less equipped to address them and less hopeful they can be solved. That residents of Metro Detroit are still debating today whether to call 1967 a "riot" or a "rebellion" is evidence we are living in a historical moment that began a half-century ago. The presumed end of the rebellion only returned the city to conditions of low-intensity warfare.[27]

The Rise of the
Counter-Revolution

In the wake of the 1967 rebellion, just as the acceleration of white flight was pushing toward a black urban majority, African American political mobilization assumed new purpose in the neighborhoods, the factories, the schools, and the streets. Above all, black Detroiters were driven to the polls in 1973 to stem the high tide of racist policing, especially in the form of the deadly and despised STRESS.

At his first inauguration in January 1974, Mayor Coleman A. Young stated that the city had "too long been polarized" and called for an end to "racial division." He emphasized the commonality of interests between white and black, between rich and poor, and he went out of his way to recognize that "what is good for those who live in the suburbs is good for those of us who live in the central city." However, his brief oration would go down in history and the permanent memory of white suburbanites for this one passage: "I issue open warnings now to all dope pushers, to all rip-off artists, to all muggers. It's time to leave Detroit. Hit Eight Mile Road."[1]

While the mayor was certainly not a man who minced words, one must wonder if anything he said in the post-rebellion climate could have effectively soothed tensions. The long road named "8 Mile" (made famous by Eminem) defines the border that separates the city of Detroit from its northern suburbs, serving as a metaphor for the social and racial divisions that have torn apart the region. What Young intended as an anticrime message in tune with the "law and order" sentiment of the day was received as a declaration of war on the suburbs.

Michel Foucault's postulate, reversing the famous aphorism of Carl von Clausewitz, that politics is war pursued by other means, is a useful lens though which to examine the post-rebellion era in metropolitan Detroit. When we look at the structures of racial oppression and segregation, it becomes evident that relations of force have ultimately sustained them over the course of Detroit history.[2]

On the surface, white flight appeared to create a racial stalemate. Black Power activists and their allies substantially redefined Detroit as a "chocolate city" where a majority black population could exert "community control" and achieve a new level of economic and political mobility. Instead, as suburbanization was combined with deindustrialization and financialization, black Detroiters found themselves surrounded and controlled by forces increasingly beyond their control. Seen from this vantage point, the policing of the rebellion was only the most visible manifestation of these relations of force.

SUBURBANIZATION AND THE RACIAL DIVIDE

For two decades, until he left office in 1994, Coleman A. Young towered over all others in Detroit's political landscape. With a long history of struggles not only as a labor and civil rights activist but also as a Tuskegee Airman, "Hizzoner" adopted a stance that was unapologetically pro-Detroit and pro-black. A fellow traveler of the Communist Party, he famously stared down the House Un-American Activities Committee during the era of McCarthyism. There was literally and figuratively a new sheriff in town. Acting on his promise to create a "people's police department," Young moved quickly to dismantle STRESS and integrate the Detroit Police Department, which was now subject to civilian oversight based on the new city charter that voters approved in 1973. Mayor Young appointed the first black police chief in 1976, and by 1978 there were black majorities on the city council and the board of education.[3]

Young's election was a transformative event within the black political world. The cultural and political imprint of the Black Power movement can still be traced through individual attitudes and community-organizing activities throughout the city, such as the Shrine of the Black Madonna and the Republic of New Africa. However, given the repression and dissolution of most radical elements, the most concrete manifestation of Black Power was the rise of African Americans within electoral politics and municipal government. Ed Vaughn, who served as a top aide to Mayor Young and was later elected to the Michigan House of Representatives, saw this as a practical advance for the movement. While it seemed "the revolution was here," he recalled, "I also felt like we were going to lose the revolution because I knew that you could not defeat tanks with bricks and that there was not enough weaponry in the community."[4]

The pride that African Americans took in the city's first black mayor found its mirror image in suburban white resentment, and Detroit became the most racially segregated major metropolitan area in the nation. Whites who had fled or planned to flee the city routinely cast Young's election as the tragic outcome of the rebellion and the death of their city as they knew it. As dissected by historian Lila Corwin Berman, Jewish suburbanization presented a complex case of white flight. While Jews remained supportive of "progressive race-neutral laws" and did not become "conservative," fissures in the liberal Jewish–African American coalition widened as the Jewish emphasis on individual rights within the capitalist order collided with black assertions of "community control" and activist governance.[5]

It is important to dispel the notion that the rebellion caused white flight. In fact, many whites had long resisted peaceful coexistence with black neighbors. For much of the 20th century, homeowners' associations functioned as organizations of white residential privilege backed by subsidies from the Federal Housing Authority and the Veteran's Administration. Furthermore, the postwar construction of the Interstate Highway System blazed a path of destruction through the heart of politically vulnerable communities of color. The freeways tore through Detroit's black business district, Paradise Valley, while facilitating white flight and capital flight to the suburbs. By 1960, the suburban population surpassed that of Detroit, and 22,000 white residents were leaving the city annually by mid-decade. Many moved to cities, such as Southfield, Grosse Pointe, and Troy, that did not have a single black-owned home.[6]

Still, there is no doubt that white flight accelerated, and did so dramatically, in the aftermath of 1967. When the rebellion broke out, there were a million whites living in Detroit; a decade later, there were roughly half as many. Eighty thousand white residents fled Detroit in 1968 alone. In the two years following the rebellion, the city of Livonia, located 15 miles west of

Downtown Detroit, hired 36 teachers from Detroit Public Schools and claimed that nearly a thousand more had applied.[7]

White flight spread in every direction, taking on particular characteristics based on the city's historical development. To the west sat Dearborn, whose growth was spurred by Henry Ford's colossal River Rouge complex, which became his company's center of operations in the late 1920s and once employed over 100,000 workers. From the 1940s to the '70s, Orville Hubbard, the infamous longtime mayor of Dearborn, declared openly and unabashedly that "niggers" were not welcome. The prominent exception to racial exclusion was the Arab American community, which was legally categorized as "white" and organized defiantly against displacement. Dearborn is now the unofficial capital of Arab America but also a national target of Islamophobia. On Detroit's eastern border sat Grosse Pointe, where the high cost of housing maintained a significant level of exclusivity; its neighborhoods also employed racial and ethnic screening processes that were more genteel than Hubbard's overt white supremacy but no less bigoted.[8]

Detroit's Eastside had been home to concentrations of working-class Catholics and "white ethnics"—descendants of industrial-era Southern and Eastern European immigration distinct from the nation's so-called Anglo-Saxon stock. These white homeowners tended to resettle in the suburbs of Macomb County northeast of Detroit. Relocation of industrial production, most notably the postwar creation of the GM Tech Center, made Warren the county's largest city and the state's second-largest city. Just across 8 Mile Road, Warren also took extreme measures to prevent black residency within its city boundaries. Much like Dearborn, 30 percent of the workforce in Warren's auto factories was African American, yet 99 percent of its 180,000 residents in 1970 were white. Warren made dubious history by turning down a $2.8 million neighborhood development grant from the U.S. Department of Housing and Urban Development (HUD) because the city would not agree to moderate steps to achieve open housing, as mandated by new regulations under President Nixon. Warren residents held vocal, angry protests against what they called "forced integration," even chasing HUD cabinet secretary (and former Michigan governor) George Romney out of town when he came to discuss the matter. Yet they were far from alone in their sentiments. In 1975, the Detroit chapter of the National Association for the Advancement of Colored People (NAACP) charged 26 suburbs that had applied for federal grants with upholding "patterns of systematic racism."[9]

As a member of the Warren City Council, Richard Sabaugh was a leader of the fight against the HUD grant in 1970. Two decades later, as a commissioner for Macomb County, he remained firm in his opinion. "It's all as one complex—blacks, Coleman Young, crime, drugs, Detroit," he said. "People feel they've been driven out once, and it could occur again." This was no slip of the tongue. Sabaugh was speaking in a formal interview as a public relations expert. "We feel that anybody coming from Detroit is going to cause problems," he added. Detroit, in his eyes, was a "completely foreign" entity that had once victimized whites, forcing them to flee, and still remained a constant threat to white suburban life.[10]

This was politics as war continued by other means, and such sentiments not only informed human relations in southeast Michigan but also remade the national political landscape. This history forces us to complicate our understanding of the political realignment commonly associated with the "Southern Strategy." Through the mid-1960s, the major parties had worked to amass eclectic groupings of support into national coalitions. Leading Democrats were southern segregationists who supported liberal government spending, while leading Republicans included northern fiscal conservatives who opposed Jim Crow. The passage of the landmark 1964 Civil Rights Act and 1965 Voting Rights Act solidified black support for the Democrats but provided the opening for the GOP to renew its appeal to white voters. While the South has since become the GOP's strongest bastion of support, historians have pointed out that realignment was not exclusive to the South but also reflected the dramatic growth of suburban populations and shifts in white suburban voting patterns.[11]

After Reagan's landslide reelection in 1984, Macomb County, a former Democrat stronghold, was viewed as ground zero for the rise of the "Reagan Democrats." Liberals initially cited the "culture of poverty" in the ghetto as a rationale for a range of social programs to uplift poor and minority communities. However, as funding and political will for "War on Poverty" programs ebbed, conservatives seized on the culture of poverty thesis as a rationale for gutting these programs in the name of ending dependency on "big government." The right wing blamed the single-mother phenomenon on the supposed loose moral standards of black girls and women, and Reagan focused scorn on the "welfare queen" he accused of cheating the taxpayers with a lazy and licentious lifestyle. These stereotypical portrayals of the "underclass" further advanced the rationale for the state to invest in policing and criminalization rather than antipoverty programs, public education, and social support. Indeed, Bill Clinton's focus on measures to end welfare and expand mass incarceration was calculated to appeal to such voters by shifting the Democratic Party to the right.

While advancing an economic agenda favoring corporations and wealthy elites, Republicans from Nixon and Reagan to Trump have successfully appealed to white voters from working families by fanning the flames of racial resentment. According to researchers Samuel Sommers and Michael Norton, since the 1960s whites have reported a growing perception that they are victims of discrimination and that minority groups are advancing at their expense. "In stark contrast to data on almost any outcome that has been assessed," they conclude, "our average white respondent believed that at the time of our survey in 2011, anti-white bias was an even bigger problem than anti-black bias." Pew Research Center reported in 2016 that only 36 percent of white Americans—and just 18 percent of Republicans—"see discrimination as a major factor holding black people back."[12]

Such attitudes have both fed and reflected the spread of anti-Detroit sentiment among suburban whites. Political scientist Stanley Greenberg conducted extensive surveys and focus groups in Macomb County in the 1980s. Although stung by factory closures and economic downturn, these voters who abandoned the Democrats linked their economic anxiety to the so-called reverse racism they believed the civil rights era had created. In their eyes, anti-discrimination measures were giving blacks special advantages over whites, and Detroit was a symbol of government handouts doled out to the undeserving poor. As it had since the days of slavery and Jim Crow, racial resentment—now filtered through fear and loathing of the inner city—served as the formula for cross-class unity among whites. Linked to disaffection that "big government" was attacking personal freedom (e.g., by attacking access to guns), the assertion of "individual rights" became the "color-blind" basis of white opposition to affirmative action and other policies based on group identity.

Even as government programs like Social Security and Medicare have remained highly popular, these cultural appeals based on individualism have worked to bind white working families to a neoliberal ideology underlying policies that intensify class stratification.[13]

In fact, the conservative economic agenda has best served the upscale suburbs in Oakland County. In the aftermath of the 1967 rebellion, Republicans there also adopted a political posture in direct opposition to the empowerment of black Detroit. While blacks were less likely to afford homes in Oakland County, white anxieties about racial integration and children's safety congealed around a proposed plan to bus public school students across the border between the city and suburbs. In response to a lawsuit filed by the NAACP, a federal judge ordered the creation of a cross-border desegregation plan that would mix the predominantly black population of Detroit Public Schools with white students from suburban schools. Like Boston, Detroit became a prime example of how the battle over integrating the schools had expanded to the North. Busing opponents contested the desegregation plan in higher courts and mobilized protest on the ground. Their efforts reached fruition in 1974, when the U.S. Supreme Court ruled cross-district busing unconstitutional in *Milliken v. Bradley*.[14]

One of the leading figures in the anti-busing movement was L. Brooks Patterson, a lawyer who parlayed his ability to arouse white emotional responses at the grassroots into a political career. Patterson was elected Oakland County executive in 1992 and is still running the county a quarter-century later. As evidence of the "business-friendly" approach, he has been an unapologetic proponent of sprawl. "I love sprawl," Patterson has declared. "I need it. I promote it. Oakland County can't get enough of it." More than a rejection of ecological sustainability, suburban sprawl serves as a color-blind euphemism for white flight. Patterson has confessed to harboring "hatred" for Detroit and believes that Coleman Young "took the city down" out of personal resentment of white racism.[15]

Suburban conservatism was further built on fears that liberals were undermining the traditional family, particularly through support of women's and LGBT rights. The concept of "family values" was more than a rallying cry of the GOP and the religious right; it became a protective shield around a suburban culture harboring sentiments that were both xenophobic and hypocritical. In June 1982, Vincent Chin was beaten to death in the middle of Woodward Avenue by two white men in one of the most discussed hate crimes in Detroit and Asian American history. Ronald Ebens wielded a baseball bat while his stepson, Michael Nitz, held Chin still. Both were from Macomb County. Nitz was a laid-off autoworker, Ebens a Chrysler foreman. "It's because of you motherfuckers that we're all out of work," Ebens yelled to Chin. In true racist fashion, he took out his xenophobic resentment of Japanese auto competition on Chin, a Chinese American raised in Michigan. The injustice took a qualitative leap further when Ebens and Nitz, after being allowed to plead guilty to manslaughter, were sentenced to just three years probation. The rationale of the judge and the killers' defenders was that they were good, family-oriented men who had randomly stumbled across Chin in an inner-city strip club. It was a rationale facilitated by the privileging of the white male patriarch as the anchor of American culture.[16]

The suburban "family values" discourse was further sustained by projecting transgressive behavior onto Detroit. For example, the problem of blighted structures became a material reality after African Americans took political power in the city. However, that does not mean that the problem should be solely pinned on Detroit's existing residents. In Downtown, 37 buildings were purchased or managed by Michael Higgins, a white man from Grosse Pointe, who became the district's worst absentee slumlord from the 1970s into the 2000s. Within residential neighborhoods, homeowners regularly abandoned homes after moving to the suburbs, and absentee landlords exploited tenants while neglecting maintenance. Some property owners commissioned arsonists to help them collect insurance payouts. In the meantime, buildings were stripped of everything from intricate ornamentation to basic copper plumbing and wiring, with the market for these stolen goods extending far beyond the city. Detroiters suffered from these patterns of behavior as much as, or more than, they were the cause of them.[17]

Drug activity within the city was also heavily linked to suburban vice. While the crack epidemic undoubtedly devastated Detroit, the racially disparate policing and criminalization inherent in the "War on Drugs" was the source of much of the damage. Studies have indicated no special propensity for drug use by Detroiters. Data from 2007 revealed significantly lower usage rates of illegal drugs among Detroit high school students, compared to nationwide averages, despite their being more likely to have drugs pushed on them. Furthermore, the *Detroit Free Press* reported that 60 percent of people arrested for drug-related offenses in Detroit between 2000 and 2002 lived outside the city. Police stated that the highest concentration of drug deals occurred near entry points to the city. A longtime resident of the Brightmoor neighborhood on the city's Westside said, "You name it, you see all kinds of cars—Mercedes, Ford 350 trucks with the extended cabs, BMWs—and the drivers are well-dressed folks."

In November 1992, the clampdown on drugs led to the widely publicized police killing of Malice Green, as the nation was still reeling from the beating of Rodney King and ensuing rebellion in Los Angeles. Green, a 35-year-old black man, was beaten to death after being stopped in his car near a suspected crack house by two white cops, Walter Budzyn and Larry Nevers. The officers had a record of abuse complaints, and one was a veteran of the notorious STRESS unit. After they were found guilty of second-degree murder, civil rights advocates breathed a sigh of relief, but the head of the police union was defiant, calling the verdicts "a victory for the drug addicts, dope dealers, pimps, and prostitutes."[18]

As legal scholar Michelle Alexander has argued, the post-rebellion calls for "law and order" expanded into a nationwide trend toward criminalization and a system of mass incarceration that set back many of the advances African Americans had made during the civil rights movement. Historian Dan Berger has called mass incarceration a repressive "response to the political crises caused by postwar revolutionary movements." Feeding a sense of moral panic, conservatives cited high crime rates and family breakups to demand cuts to social welfare programs and an emphasis on harsher policing and stricter punishment, much of which was conducted under the banner of the War on Drugs. Both Democrats and Republicans ultimately embraced key elements of the carceral state. Leading the world in rate of incarceration, the United States went from holding fewer than 350,000 persons in prisons and jails in 1972 to more than 2 million in recent years. In response to counter-revolutionary grassroots pressure and perverse federal incentives, Michigan now spends more money on young people in prison than in schools. By 2009, one of every 25 adults in Detroit—and one out of seven in some parts of the Eastside—was under correctional control: a total of

24,272 persons, including 10,882 in prison, at an annual cost of nearly $400 million. The impact has been widespread. As Ruth Wilson Gilmore remarks, "Prisons wear out places by wearing out people, irrespective of whether they have done time."[19]

With mainstream discourse defining the bucolic, family-friendly suburb in opposition to the drug- and crime-infested city, suburbanization transformed the cultural and political landscape of Detroit. The black pursuit of "community control" to obtain a "fair share" of Detroit's economic pie turned into a zero-sum game with the suburbs, which intensified as regional economic growth tapered off. By 1980, Detroit was two-thirds black, while the suburbs were 88 percent white and had nearly double the city's population. From 1970 to 2000, an estimated 160,000 homes in Detroit were abandoned by their owners; median home values fell from $67,000 to $62,000 within the city but rose from $94,000 to $142,000 in the suburbs. Conservatives in the suburbs blamed the city for its own problems, and they embraced Reagan's call to end "big government." All the while, they continued to demand the infrastructure and federal subsidies—including FHA and VA mortgages and IRS deductions for mortgage interest—needed to facilitate sprawl.[20]

DEINDUSTRIALIZATION AND
THE TWO-TIERED SOCIETY

Because the local ascendancy of black political power coincided with the rollback of liberal fiscal policy, Detroit's post-1967 African American leadership class quickly realized the limits of "community control" to replicate the patterns of white upward mobility into the middle class. As the auto companies at the center of Detroit's economy went into a tailspin, the impact on the city was abrupt and devastating. During the 1970s, Detroit lost one-fifth of its population, as nearly a quarter-million jobs evaporated from the city. By the early 1980s, black unemployment in the city soared to 34 percent, and Detroit had the largest income disparity between the central city and suburbs of any major metropolitan region in the United States.[21]

Despite Young's penchant for in-your-face rhetoric, his actual governing policies were relatively moderate and his fiscal policy was surprisingly conservative. Beyond any of his peers since 1950, as reported by the *Detroit Free Press,* Young slashed budgets and laid off thousands of workers "to preside over a city with more income than debt."[22]

For many Detroit activists, including DRUM founder and city council member Ken Cockrel Sr., the mayor's biggest shortcoming was that he was too pliant with the auto industry and the city's corporate employers. Young was quick to offer massive subsidies to meet their needs. In his eyes, it was the only option to retain jobs in a time of government cutbacks and weakening unions. Two of the city's biggest investments, however, offered questionable returns. In 1981, to meet GM's demands for a new factory in Detroit, the city spent $200 million to claim most of the Poletown neighborhood through eminent domain, displacing 150 businesses and 4,000 residents, some of whom resisted to the bitter end. In addition to the land and infrastructure, GM received $120 million in tax abatements. All this effort went toward producing 3,000 new jobs in the highly automated Poletown plant; at the same time, GM closed two plants that had employed 10,000 workers. A decade later, the city buckled to Chrysler's demands for aid to modernize its Jefferson plant on the Eastside, providing subsidies that were projected to cost the city $245 million over 20 years.[23]

The mayor also prioritized the development of Downtown, partnering with Henry Ford II and the corporate leaders who built the Renaissance Center (first pushed by Mayor Gribbs) in the 1970s. Many in this group had formed a coalition dubbed New Detroit in the aftermath of the rebellion, issuing audacious statements that raised expectations within the city that some kind of public-private Marshall Plan would emerge. But the shift in focus to "Detroit Renaissance" was a retreat from the social arena, drawing the development schemes more firmly into the business world. In fact, the Renaissance Center, with its massive amounts of unused and underutilized space and its fortress-like design, proved to be a major flop both culturally and economically. Mayor Young, nonetheless, continued to insist that working with white corporate leaders was essential to his duties. "Ain't no black people wielding any of the major power—economic power—in this city," he once remarked.[24]

The Big Three auto companies, however, were shrinking along with the city. A half-century ago, GM was the nation's largest employer. In jobs that generally didn't require a college degree, workers made an average of $35 an hour (in today's dollars). The managed bankruptcies of GM and Chrysler during the Great Recession, accompanied by a parallel restructuring of Ford, cemented an end to the standard of wages and benefits the United Auto Workers (UAW) had secured during the boom years of the mid-20th century. The union had suffered serious blows during the late 1970s and early '80s, when the oil crisis hit and Chrysler nearly went bankrupt. Not only did the UAW lose 125,000 members between 1979 and 1983, but it acknowledged the need to concede "givebacks" to the employers; in other words, the workers returned raises and benefits they had won through collective bargaining to help prop up the Big Three.[25]

The intervening boom of the 1990s, when cheap oil spurred massive profits through minivan and SUV sales, added to the problems of sprawl but were a momentary uptick in the overall downward trend for labor. The North American Free Trade Agreement eliminated duties on cars imported from Mexico, facilitating production and investment in new plants across the border. Even as the quality of American cars improved and productivity surged, the Big Three reported that their labor costs exceeded those of global competitors because they were forced to pay for health insurance, a government-sponsored benefit in the rest of the industrialized world. Conservative opponents of the union called for mass wage cuts. *Detroit News* columnist Thomas Bray argued that the "premium pay" of UAW workers was a primary source of "Detroit's welfare mentality" that continued to "hook people on the idea of something for nothing."[26]

Championed by Democrats and criticized by Republicans, the 2008–09 auto bailout neither benefited workers nor stymied free market principles to the extent either party claimed. By the 21st century, downsizing, automation, and outsourcing had already taken a major toll on the Big Three's U.S. workforce. The automakers had well-established patterns of outsourcing production to cheaper and nonunion parts suppliers across the globe. Thus, even the shrinking percentage of cars stamped "Made in America" should more accurately have been labeled "final assembly in a U.S. plant." Furthermore, the UAW workers made major concessions in negotiations preceding the bailout. In 2007, the Big Three instituted a two-tiered wage system in which new workers were hired with reduced benefits at $14 an hour—compared to the standard wage of $28. Moreover, the UAW conceded the end of guaranteed health-care benefits for retirees by accepting a one-time payment from the automakers to establish a health-care trust fund.[27]

In a *New York Times* op-ed in November 2008, Mitt Romney called on Congress to reject the bailout under the infamous headline "Let Detroit Go Bankrupt." The political price he paid for that stance—losing nearly every Rust Belt state in the 2012 presidential election—was largely for naught. In fact, the auto bailout and companion bankruptcies of GM and Chrysler gutted wages and benefits in exactly the ways Romney desired. The bailout was at best a form of "trickle-down economics" for autoworkers, with none of the money invested directly in the city. It was a lite version of Detroit's municipal bankruptcy proceedings to come.[28]

FINANCIALIZATION AND THE LOOMING CRISIS

The deindustrialization of Detroit has been a heightened case of the nation's shift away from an economy rooted in manufacturing to one dictated by finance. Since 1980, the financial sector's contribution to the U.S. gross domestic product has grown from 4 to 7 percent. While creating only 4 percent of all jobs, it commands roughly 25 percent of all corporate profits. The growth of finance capital surged exponentially after Congress and President Clinton moved in 1999 to repeal regulations in the Glass-Steagall Act that were intended to stem the financial turmoil of the Great Depression. In short, traditional banks were allowed to move beyond conventional, tangible investments to pursue high-flying Wall Street deals and high-stakes gambling on the direction of the market itself.[29]

The loosening of credit became a source of temporary relief for households feeling squeezed by rising prices and stagnating wages. Indeed, Wall Street seemed to offer solutions not only for consumers, but also for major public institutions, which made riskier investments with endowments, pension funds, and sovereign wealth funds as they desperately sought ways to accomplish more with less. Before it popped, the housing bubble became a central source of both access to credit for consumers and windfall profits for Wall Street. To spur demand for its products, the banking industry aggressively marketed $1.4 trillion in subprime mortgages; these were next churned into $14 trillion worth of securities and packaged assets sold between 2002 and 2007. High-risk, predatory mortgages were packaged and repackaged into bonds with phony high-grade ratings. It took negligence, deceit, and malice on a grand conspiratorial scale to create the global house of cards.[30]

Alongside the auto industry crisis, the housing foreclosure and banking crises fed both directly and indirectly into Detroit's bankruptcy. A total of 139,699 properties—36 percent of all the properties in the city—went into foreclosure from 2005 to 2014. The city and its housing market were already reeling from a 1999 state law outlawing residency requirements for municipal workers. Consultants estimated that the latter was costing the city $21 million in annual revenue, but more than that, it triggered another abrupt wave of white and middle-class flight. Three-fourths of Detroit's police force, including nearly all white officers, now live outside the city. The foreclosure crisis further devastated homeowners, wiping out much of the wealth of Detroit residents and taking a huge toll on the city's property tax base. It wreaked havoc on entire neighborhoods as the value of surrounding homes plummeted. The city's median home sale price had sunk to $7,000 by 2009 (and "recovered" to $30,000 by 2015). Abandoned structures became targets for illicit activities and arson, and population loss precipitated school and park closures.[31]

A class-action lawsuit against investment bank Morgan Stanley, filed in 2012 by five black Detroiters in conjunction with the American Civil Liberties Union and Michigan Legal Services, provides a window into the devastating effects of predatory lending on homeowners and neighborhoods. The lawsuit accused Morgan Stanley, acting through a now defunct mortgage broker named New Century Mortgage Company, of targeting "African-American communities and borrowers in the Detroit area" for loans with onerous terms that deliberately defied "sound underwriting practices."[32]

For decades, communities of color had their access to credit restricted by "redlining," in which government agencies and private lenders deemed nonwhite neighborhoods unsafe for investment. Facing public pressure to reverse these practices, banks pushed "exotic" loans, with usurious rates and terms, on low-income urban communities. For instance, home buyers who would not otherwise qualify for mortgages were lured with minimal or no down-payment requirement. Furthermore, monthly payments were set artificially low by "teaser" interest rates and negative amortization (whereby borrowers make such minimal payments that the total amount they owe increases as time goes on). On top of manipulative marketing and sales, mortgage brokers and lenders often trafficked in outright lies, encouraging applicants to list incomes far above what they actually earned and basing home values on inflated appraisals.[33]

To be certain, these shady practices could be found throughout the industry, and many white upper-income-earners used them to buy homes beyond their means. The Detroit complaint, however, presented statistical evidence of racial disparity. Between 2004 and 2007, New Century sold nearly 10 times as many high-cost loans (4,291) as it did non-high-cost loans to

African Americans in Detroit. As a result, blacks made up only 21.8 percent of the company's non-high-cost business but 44.3 percent of its volume of high-cost loans. By 2008, when the fore-closure crisis was just starting to take off, 35.7 percent of the homes purchased or refinanced with New Century mortgages were already in foreclosure (the current figure is likely at least double that).[34]

The case is still active, and Morgan Stanley has denied the charge of racially discriminatory predatory lending. What is not in doubt, however, is the extent to which its employees and leaders knew something was wrong. They sent emails referring to the sub-prime mortgages as "crap" and "a bunch of scaaaarrryyyy loans!!!!!!" Morgan Stanley's head of the trading desk, Steven J. Shapiro, noted in April 2006 that the firm was likely to see "a good percentage of the borrowers going into extended delinquency/liquidation." Nonetheless, the loans were still of value to Morgan Stanley so long as they could be packaged into bonds and peddled to others, perhaps even their own clients. In response to a slew of separate complaints regarding fraudulent investment practices, Morgan Stanley agreed in February 2016 to pay over $5 billion in fines lev-ied by the U.S. Justice Department and other state and federal agencies for the firm's misconduct in residential mortgage-backed securities dealings.[35]

The global financial meltdown terrified ruling elites to such a degree that Washington actually managed to find bipartisan sup-port to pass the Emergency Economic Stabilization Act of 2008. More commonly known as the federal "bailout," the law paved the way for $3 trillion in investments, the majority of which was devoted to propping up financial markets and the financial indus-try. The $80 billion committed to the auto bailout was but a frac-tion of the overall sum. With the Federal Reserve greasing the wheels of finance with hundreds of millions in nearly interest-free money, the big banks and corporations returned to the path of financialization. When the bill came due for the City of Detroit, the high-end estimate of the city's long-term debt and unfunded obligations was only one-fourth the cost of the auto bailout. Washington, however, was in no mood to jump into the fray. "Detroit had the misfortune to go bankrupt about two years too late," said Ron Bloom, who helped lead the Obama administration's task force on the auto bailout. By 2013, "bailouts were passé."[36]

With high concentrations of poverty and rapidly aging housing stock, Detroit found itself shorthanded in both the high-stakes game of finance and the regional tug-of-war. No matter how one characterizes that war, its casualties were real and mounting: wealth evaporated, neighborhoods decayed, and inequality grew. The persistence of structural unemployment has placed Detroit in the unenviable position of topping all major American cities for rates of joblessness. In 2014, only 53 percent of Detroit residents of working age reported having been employed at any point in the prior year. Although this was far below the 75 percent U.S. average, Detroit is at the front end of national trends. The U.S. rate of male participation in the labor force has been declining since the 1950s and now ranks near the absolute bottom of all developed countries.[37]

Retreating from liberal reform, the federal government offered no panacea to Detroit, while the Big Three demanded tribute for their continued presence in the city. Ultimately, the city found itself at the mercy of state government. If 1980s Detroit had been viewed, through a dystopian lens, as a hostile foreign nation, by 2013 the financial crisis had rendered it a failed state that would have to be reoccupied.

THREE

The System Is Bankrupt

In 2011, Michigan lawmakers laid the foundation for an enhanced state takeover of Detroit and other municipalities and school districts. When first passed in 1990, "emergency management" had been limited to financial matters, but the new emergency manager law, Michigan Public Act 4, authorized the state to seize control of all matters of city governance. Within school districts, emergency managers would now control every decision regarding finances, academics, curriculum, and teaching. Reflecting the law's conservative authorship, the emergency manager could break union contracts but not cancel agreements with banks.[1]

The GOP fought ruthlessly against any attempt to contest the controversial law. After citizens collected over 200,000 signatures to subject it to a voter referendum, a conservative political action committee tied it up for months in state hearings and fought a legal case all the way to the state supreme court, based on the erroneous claim that the petition text was less than a millimeter shy of the legally required "14-point type."[2]

In November 2012, voters struck down the law by a five-point margin statewide. Republicans, however, remained unfazed. On the surface, Michigan appeared to be a solidly "blue" state. Barack Obama defeated Michigan-born Mitt Romney by 10 points, and Senator Debbie Stabenow, a Democrat, won by more than 20 points. However, at the state-government level, Michigan had become solidly "red." Even though Democrats outnumber Republicans in Michigan, and their candidates for state legislature have regularly attracted as many or more votes overall across the state, they are a beleaguered minority. By controlling redistricting, the GOP created gerrymandered districts that concentrated people of color and Democrats into as few districts as possible. The upshot was to render the vast majority of political races noncompetitive, with Republicans maintaining a commanding 63–47 majority in the House and an outlandish 27–11 majority in the Senate. This form of neutralizing the impact of voting has become an increasingly prominent civil rights issue nationwide, as well as the focus of intense legal scrutiny and court battles in other "purple" states like North Carolina with clear GOP majorities.[3]

The Michigan legislature wasted little time in passing a new emergency manager law during the lame-duck session in December 2012. This time, it made sure to add technical provisions rendering the law immune to revocation by citizen referendum. The law was officially named the Local Financial Stability and Choice Act (Michigan Public Act 436), although the effective choices it allows cities (or school districts) are largely variations on relinquishing local powers and granting state control. Public Act 436 put an exclamation point on a blizzard of conservative legislation passed during this lame-duck session to make Michigan a right-to-work state, impose severe restrictions on abortion, slash funding for social programs, rapidly advance the privatization of education and public services, and lift the ban on concealed weapons in schools. Governor Rick Snyder, the venture capitalist and CEO who had campaigned as a moderate Republican, signed all of these into law except one. With the nation still mourning the victims of the Sandy Hook Elementary School massacre, he had the decency to veto the guns-in-schools bill.[4]

The stage was set for Detroit to be taken over several months later by a Snyder-appointed emergency manager, Kevyn Orr, and then plunged into bankruptcy in July 2013. The ensuing downsizing of city government, part of Detroit's makeover by corporate lawyers and financial consultants, was consistent with Snyder's fiscally conservative philosophy and his goal of creating a more "business-friendly" environment. Because such austerity measures were unpalatable to elected officials who must answer to voters, they were carried out in an autocratic, top-down manner that Michigan's legislature had gone to extraordinary lengths to facilitate. This stupefying turn of events exemplified what author Naomi Klein has called the "shock doctrine," whereby financial crises are exploited by neoliberal elites to impose a form of "disaster capitalism" that intensifies dispossession and disenfranchisement of those in vulnerable social positions.[5]

GIVING CREDIT WHERE CREDIT IS DUE

The restructuring of the auto industry and the bankruptcy of Detroit built on various forms of retrenchment dating back to the 1970s. These efforts to rewrite the rules of the economy and public policy have defined the neoliberal era. Most noticeably to the general public, the median wage of workers effectively stagnated. Forty years ago, the top executives of major corporations received, on average, 20 times the compensation of the typical worker. In recent years, the differential has skyrocketed to nearly 300 times. Neoliberalism has not only reversed the social leveling that marked the New Deal order; it has also produced a discourse in which the representatives of the 1 percent ("the makers") deliver scolding lectures arguing that the working class and poor ("the takers") are overcompensated and getting too many handouts from the government.[6]

In basic material terms, neoliberalism has meant the vigorous assertion of corporate power, unleashed by the loosening of government regulations and the weakening of workers' rights and collective bargaining. The expansion of "free trade" has been central to the neoliberal project; however, it is better understood as the free mobility of capital to cross borders and claim private ownership over resources previously belonging to the public commons. Corporate flexibility has been strengthened by outsourcing, automation, union busting, casualization (replacing full-time workers with seasonal and part-time workers), and access to the globalized labor market. Workers, however, have seen their mobility restricted most literally by national borders but also figuratively by domestic laws and international agreements designed to give employers the upper hand in the name of stimulating "investment."

Neoliberalism is far more than a set of economic policies. It is an ideology that leads to unfounded assumptions that the public sector is inherently wasteful and that the private sector always has a better, more cost-efficient way to carry out a task, whether we are talking about garbage collection or the education of our children. And it is an ideology that refuses to acknowledge its own hypocrisy, insisting that homeowners in foreclosure and pensioners in distressed municipalities must learn a stern lesson in frugality but that the big banks tallying gambling losses in the billions are "too big to fail" and must be propped up by government largesse. The two-tiered society has created two different sets of rules to coincide with its gaping wealth gap.

As the economic squeeze of the 1970s led consumers to take on increasing debt, municipalities were concordantly pushed to borrow to make ends meet. A reliance on credit from the municipal bond market left the fate of cities increasingly entangled with Wall Street. This weakening of financial independence further rendered local governments vulnerable to the political machinations of the 1 percent. New York and other cities stood at the center of a nationwide budget crisis when the first wave of neoliberal restructuring emerged in the 1970s. And while the black political class exercised "community control," the global balance of power was shifting rightward. Military forces allied with the interests of national elites and global capital toppled governments of nations—including Chile, which had democratically elected socialist president Salvador Allende—or repressed the progressive opposition.[7]

Geographer David Harvey argues that "a coup d'état by financial institutions" accomplished similar economic goals by attaching harsh strings to the bailout of New York City in 1975. "This meant," he notes, "curbing the aspirations of municipal unions, layoffs in public employment, wage freezes, cutbacks in social provision (education, public health, and transport services), and the imposition of user fees (tuition was introduced in the CUNY university system for the first time)." Harvey asserts that this settlement established as principle that "the integrity of financial institutions and bondholders" took precedence over "the well-being of the citizens" and "hammered home the view that the role of government was to create a good business climate." This became the national standard for fiscal austerity measures set by the Reagan administration during the 1980s. The International Monetary Fund (IMF) made it the global standard by imposing onerous agreements that fostered continued borrowing but little hope of restoring financial health for nations of the Global South beset by interconnected oil, inflation, and debt crises.[8]

Although Detroit felt the adverse affects of the paradigm shift toward austerity, Coleman Young's fiscal conservatism kept the threat of insolvency at arm's length. Detroit's financial health and bond rating, however, took a series of severe hits under his successors. From 2002 to 2012, Detroit's funding from state revenue sharing, in which cities received an annual portion of sales taxes collected by the state, plummeted from $334 million to $173 million. The city's advocates charged the state legislature with reneging on a 1999 agreement between Governor John Engler and Mayor Dennis Archer that guaranteed revenue sharing after the city agreed to cut its income tax rate. The funding cuts compounded the city's economic woes as the dot-com and SUV-buying bubbles of the 1990s began to burst.[9]

Decades of hardship gave the banks leverage to reduce Detroit's options to "heads we win, tails you lose" propositions. Nevertheless, if there was one poison pill that most triggered the city's financial insolvency, it was the 2005 plan to borrow $1.44 billion, which amounted to little more than a Ponzi scheme. Looking for creative ways to fund its pension obligations without enacting devastating budget cuts and layoffs, Mayor Kwame Kilpatrick's administration found willing partners on Wall Street, which was peddling newfangled schemes made possible by deregulation. Instead of paying the money necessary to keep the retirement funds of municipal workers secure, the city government participated in a deliberately complex plan devised to skirt laws and regulations. To create a paper fiction that it was not exceeding the legal limit for municipal debt, the city created a new trust, effectively a shell corporation, to take on the new debt by selling "pension obligation certificates of participation." Next, Detroit purchased "interest rate swaps" from UBS and Merrill Lynch (later absorbed by Bank of America) that locked in an interest rate of 6 percent. Finally, the city purchased insurance on the bonds and more interest rate swaps from two other Wall Street entities.[10]

Kilpatrick vowed the unprecedented plan would save the city $80 million that year and $277 million over the next 14 years. Instead, the pension bond plan collapsed like a house of cards, epitomizing the sophisticated but ethically challenged financial dealings that were at the center of the global meltdown in 2008. Not only did it fail to save the city money, the $1.44 billion pension bond plan ultimately put the municipal government on the hook for 22 years of principal, interest, and insurance payments totaling $2.8 billion (as assessed at the time Detroit declared bankruptcy in 2013). Because interest rates plummeted, the city wound up paying for the privilege of locking in a relatively high interest rate and was increasingly strapped just to make payments on the swaps, let alone the original bond debt. Hence, Detroit borrowed still more money, on even less desirable terms. This debt balloon was the single biggest cause of Detroit's reportedly looming default that triggered the state takeover.[11]

What the pension bond fiasco perfectly symbolized was the warped lens through which elites in media and politics have framed the city's crisis. By the time Governor Snyder gave Kevyn Orr autocratic power to run the city as an emergency manager, former mayor Kilpatrick was languishing in prison on a 28-year sentence, having been convicted of multiple crimes and branded a liar, thief, and philanderer in the court of public opinion. The "hip hop mayor" was thus a more than convenient scapegoat for a financial scheme that in hindsight looks foolish, corrupt, and scandalous.

The pension bond deal, however, could not be attributed to the antics of a disgraced mayor. It was hatched on Wall Street and facilitated by Kilpatrick's chief financial officer, Sean Werdlow, who subsequently landed a plum job at one of the key investment banks that engineered the deal. What linked this practice to the predatory consumer lending underlying the home foreclosure crisis was the immediate, shortsighted profit motive: financial firms collected fees on the transactions up front, without worrying about the actual quality of the loans, since they were destined to be resold anyway. When emergency management began in March 2013, reporters from Bloomberg calculated that Detroit had paid $474 million in Wall Street fees just for the servicing of its debt—in other words, not even counting the interest paid on the debt itself. Amid a flood of such deals, Wall Street had singled out Detroit's pension bond plan as creative and innovative. Indeed, it went so far as to honor Kwame Kilpatrick at a black-tie gala in Manhattan, where Detroit was awarded the Midwest Regional Deal of the Year award from the *Bond Buyer* newspaper.[12]

The much-maligned Detroit City Council provided the only outlet for citizens to take a stand against putting the city's fate in the hands of Wall Street financiers. However, city council members who questioned the deal and called for alternatives were browbeaten into going along with it. Dismissing their opposition as dim-witted and calling them "a threat to the stability of the community they were elected to represent," the *Detroit Free Press* editorial board blithely assured the public that "the restructuring of pension obligations is a sound plan, akin to refinancing a mortgage at lower rates." At a key point in the debate, the city even tried to force the reluctant council members to meet and vote on the plan by ordering the police to round them up. These were stunning displays of how neoliberal orthodoxy, however unsound and illegal, came to be seen as commonsense through a combination of coercion and consent. None of the council members who properly raised suspicions about the plan in 2005 hold office today. Regardless, when the emergency manager took over, the popularly elected officials were neutralized, so the financiers could finish the job they started.[13]

WHAT'S BAD FOR DETROIT IS BAD FOR AMERICA

Detroit was far from the first Michigan city to be placed under emergency management, although it fit a disturbing pattern. Flint was taken over by the state in 2002 and again by Governor Snyder under the enhanced law in 2011. When the state took control of Detroit, it became one of six cities under emergency management, comprising 9 percent of the state's total population. These six cities, however, were home to roughly half of Michigan's black residents.[14]

Flint became the center of a national scandal after its emergency manager, in a presumed cost-cutting measure, ordered a shift to the polluted Flint River for the city's drinking water between 2013 and 2014. For 18 months, Flint's entire population of over 100,000 people, 60 percent African American, was poisoned by toxic water. When residents, supported by scientists and doctors, came forward with evidence of brown water that smelled foul and burned their skin, state government officials arrogantly disregarded complaints, suffering, and death as the disaster in Flint spread for months. Although Flint went back to having Detroit supply its water, the residual damage has made unfiltered tap water undrinkable as of this writing. Moreover, although Flint's government was nominally restored in April 2015, it remains tethered to the dictates of an oversight board appointed by Governor Snyder. In March 2016, the state removed the city's autonomy to initiate litigation, specifically to preclude Flint from suing the state over the damage caused by the water fiasco. Flint's residents are thus left questioning the extent to which there will be true accountability.[15]

Alongside Detroit, Flint became emblematic of how a system producing greater and greater inequality—to the point where basic needs for health and safety can no longer be met—has sought to preserve order by disenfranchising citizens who are black and poor. This is an extension of voter-suppression tactics deployed throughout the nation. Because Republicans have failed to attract voters of color, the GOP has simply tried to impede them by making it difficult to register, removing voters from the rolls, and imposing strict ID requirements to cast a ballot. Ironically, the appointment of Detroit's emergency manager occurred as the Supreme Court was debating (and eventually weakening) the Voting Rights Act, which Justice Scalia characterized as the "perpetuation of racial entitlement." Following the extremely close 2016 presidential election, irregularities and voting-machine malfunctions, which were discovered before Michigan's state recount was shut down, further intensified concerns about voting rights and procedures.[16]

It is the combination of fiscal austerity measures and political disenfranchisement—both pushed to new extremes—that has created a dangerous precedent in Detroit. The Flint fiasco has led Snyder and Republican leaders to become even more invested in portraying Detroit's emergency management regime as a success. When Attorney General Bill Schuette charged two former Flint emergency managers with crimes that could result in 46-year prison sentences, he declared that "a fixation on finances and balance sheets" had resulted in the deadly prioritization of "numbers over people, money over health." What happened in Flint, however, was not a perversion of the autocratic emergency management law—it was a highly foreseeable conclusion. The "fixation on finances and balance sheets" was built into the job requirement of the emergency managers. It was the main justification for Snyder singularly focusing on hiring a corporate bankruptcy lawyer to run Detroit.[17]

Conservatives seized on Detroit's bankruptcy to condemn what they saw as the failures of the public sector, while calling for cutting budgets, curtailing the power of unions, and boosting privatization. In some cases, they openly hailed the elimination of local autonomy and democratic rule. George Will argued that Detroit's bankruptcy signified "death by democracy." The failure of "self-government" in Detroit, Will asserted, posed "worrisome questions about the viability of democracy in jurisdictions where big government and its unionized employees collaborate in pillaging taxpayers."[18]

Left-of-center national commentators asserted that Detroit's economic crisis not only disproportionately harmed African Americans, but was itself a product of racism. Cultural critic Andrew O'Hehir compared Detroit's slide into bankruptcy to the negligence witnessed in New Orleans, a comparable black metropolis, as the floodwaters of Katrina rose. The nation looked "like a bitter, miserly and dying empire where the deluded rich cling to their McMansions and mock the suffering of the poor while everyone else fights over the scraps." Historian Thomas Sugrue drew attention to the "very strong racial dimension" driving the "intense hostility between the city and the rest of the state." Republicans in Lansing had "mostly been elected by voters who are profoundly suspicious of Detroit, who see it as a sinkhole, a corrupt Third-World country, emblem of urban misrule."[19]

Almost as if on cue, L. Brooks Patterson—Oakland County's chief executive and one of the region's most powerful suburban politicians for over two decades—added fuel to the fire with an instantly notorious interview published by the *New Yorker.* Patterson stated common, panic-stricken stereotypes about the city as dangerous: "You do not, do not, under any circumstances, stop in Detroit at a gas station. That's just a call for a carjacking." Using explicitly racial discourse, Patterson asserted the city would never recover from its economic crisis: "I made a prediction a long time ago, and it's come to pass. I said, 'What we're gonna do is turn Detroit into an Indian reservation, where we herd all the Indians into the city, build a fence around it, and then throw in the blankets and corn.'" This time Patterson not only outraged Detroiters but sparked protest by Native Americans throughout the region. Patterson's race-baiting shtick folds neatly into the white nationalism, Islamophobia, and anti-Semitism stirred up by Trump's election. Still, with Oakland County beginning to tilt Democratic, it may finally be wearing out its welcome with his increasingly ethnically diverse constituency.[20]

The most concerted opposition to the emergency management regime came from a coalition of 35 groups, including churches, civil rights organizations, legal advocates, and community activists addressing issues ranging from education to poverty. Under the banner of Detroiters Resisting Emergency Management, the coalition denounced the governor's appointment of managers who were handed "dictatorial powers to advance the interests of banks and private corporations over the public good." It was "one of the most ruthlessly racist maneuvers in U.S. contemporary politics." Releasing a "people's plan" delineating a set of alternative policies and principles, the coalition called for addressing the structural roots of the city's crisis and putting the interests of poor people and communities of color first. The opening lines of the manifesto proclaimed:

> The restructuring and rebirth of Detroit will not be delivered by a state-imposed emergency manager, nor through Chapter 9 bankruptcy proceedings, foundation contributions, closed door deals, or other devious and misleading corporate schemes. Detroit's rebirth will be the result of the people's unrelenting demand for democratic self-governance, equal access to and management of the natural and economic resources of the city.[21]

THE NEW NORMAL

Proponents of the state takeover orchestrated David Harvey's equivalent of a financial "coup" to impose austerity measures that they deemed too unpopular for elected officials to embrace. Those who saw Detroit as a symbol of bloated government placed much of the blame on the power of public-sector unions, which George Will likened to the parasitical larvae of the ichneumon fly—only to conclude that the unions are actually worse than the parasite. Right-to-work legislation had already promised to frustrate private-sector union organizers, and the UAW had, in many ways, been reduced to a junior partner of the Big Three. Detroit's municipal bankruptcy became an opportunity to gut the impact of public-sector unions—already a target of conservative political activism in Wisconsin and elsewhere, owing to the outsized influence they were seen as having within electoral politics.

Detroit's emergency manager asserted that the unions had "imposed work rules and other restrictions that impaired the efficient functioning of City government." Among the "onerous" rules he cited were staffing "based solely on seniority, rather than merit, qualifications or experience" and contractual "limitations on management rights and responsibilities." Corporate consultants were thus brought in to reduce labor costs and enhance the flexibility of management. However, what emergency manager Kevyn Orr and the private consultants called, from the viewpoint of employers, "restrictions" translated to security for workers against arbitrary treatment, discipline, and firing. They were especially important to African American and other nonwhite workers who saw subjective standards and top-down management practices as invitations to discriminate.[22]

Orr used the power of his office and the implicit threat of abrogating union contracts as a cudgel to bring the unions on board with his final plan of adjustment, which, he later asserted, would save the city $200 million annually in labor-related costs. As in the case of the auto industry, the restructuring would deliberately roll back decades of bargaining leverage and material gains—consequences organizers would be forced to wrestle with for years. In the short term, however, the battle within the bankruptcy proceedings was focused on slashing retiree pensions and health-care benefits—a direct blow to the cumulative achievements of collective bargaining.[23]

Emergency Manager Orr initially took a firm negotiating stance, seeking to nearly eliminate the debt owed to all the city's creditors. But what constitutes a creditor? By pure accounting,

retirees expecting pensions fell under the same category of
creditor as Wall Street banks that were owed money for bad
derivative wagers, in the simple sense that the city was obligated
to make payments to both. Orr argued that his obligation to
Detroit was to reduce the city's debt as much as possible, regardless of whether the banks or the pensioners would take a haircut.
He estimated a $3.5 billion shortfall in the funds dedicated to
32,427 pensioners. The average pension for a city worker was
$19,213. For police and fire department employees it was $30,607,
though these pensions made them ineligible for social security.
Neither provided funds to live lavishly. Nevertheless, Orr's initial plan proposed reducing payments for current pensioners as
much as 90 percent while ending cost-of-living adjustments,
severely reducing health-care benefits, and moving current
workers to a defined-contribution, 401(k)-style plan. He characterized his strategy as offering "a sincere olive branch," but he
warned, "I can cut somebody's throat and leave them to bleed
out in the gutter with the best of them."[24]

Critics asserted it was wrong to lump the banks and pensioners together. For starters, legal representatives of the pensioners
argued that the Michigan State Constitution forbids cuts to
public pensions. The governor sharply disagreed. "The constitution does not say you have a guaranteed right to a pension,"
Snyder argued. "It says it's an accrued financial benefit that's a
contractual obligation. Bankruptcy is really the ability to abro-
gate a contractual right."[25]

Beyond legalities, supporters of the pensioners made a moral
and political case for prioritizing the needs of the human beings
whose fixed-income retirement was based on pension payments
they assumed were guaranteed. Paulette Brown, a retiree from
the sewage plant, testified before the bankruptcy court. "Many of

my coworkers worked in hazardous areas, extreme heat, extreme cold, and unsanitary conditions," she stated. "We all breathed in air filled with the smell of feces and raw sewage on a daily basis. We went above and beyond the call of duty. We fulfilled our agreement with the City of Detroit, and for that, upon retirement we receive medical benefits and a pension based on an agreed-upon formula for the rest of our lives."[26]

The outcry from the pensioners grew louder when Orr announced his first proposed settlement with Wall Street creditors. In October 2013, just before the filing of Detroit's bankruptcy, Orr arranged a deal for the city to borrow $350 million in new funds from Barclay's, primarily to pay off Bank of America and UBS (the proverbial "Swiss bank account" provider) for the bad bet on the interest rate swaps tied to the pension bond plan. While he was demanding that the pensioners take 10 cents on the dollar, Orr proposed to pay off the banks at 75 to 82 cents on the dollar. Unbelievably, he argued with confidence that he "got the best deal available" from the banks. Putting the banks first in line was a common assumption among the neoliberal architects of the bankruptcy. Since serving as the key financial strategist of Detroit's bankruptcy, Kenneth Buckfire has argued as a matter of principle that Puerto Rico should pay off its secured Wall Street debt at 100 percent while possibly wiping out its pensions entirely.[27]

However, activists and some media commentators questioned Orr's judgment, which seemed to grant "preferential treatment to these banks" and thus defeat the purpose of declaring bankruptcy. Furthermore, the three banks involved in the deal had done nothing to earn the people's good will; indeed, all had been implicated in major financial scandals, particularly for manipulating interest rates. In other words, they were swaying the outcome of Wall Street wagers like the very interest rate swaps that devastated Detroit's financial condition. The fines they and other banks agreed to pay for their role in the global financial melt-down seemed just to be the cost of doing business. In fact, the $20 billion the banking industry paid itself in bonuses for 2012 alone was enough to pay off all of Detroit's long-term debt and fund all of its long-term obligations with no reductions.[28]

So ready were Orr and his advisors to implement a private-sector restructuring model, they failed to take seriously public regulations and laws governing the city as a public entity, until ordered to do so by the court. Judge Steven Rhodes twice admon-ished Orr for being too soft on the banks. Down from the original offer of 75–82 percent, Orr ultimately settled with the banks for 30 cents on the dollar. This was still close to the 34 percent pay-out for unsecured bondholders, even though the swaps deal could have been entirely voided at the risk of a court showdown.[29]

Meanwhile, Orr significantly upped his offer to the pension-ers, offering to continue paying municipal retirees as much as 74 percent of the pension payments they are due from the city, with retired police officers and firefighters (paid from a sepa-rately managed and better endowed fund) retaining as much as 96 percent of their pensions. This was central to the "Grand Bargain," formed in response to national outrage over the fear that rarefied masterpieces in the Detroit Institute of Arts would be auctioned off to pay bondholders. Syncora and FGIC, two financial firms insuring Detroit's bad debt, had demanded that Orr put a price tag on the art to increase the potential payout to creditors. It was a shrewd legal move that backfired poli-tically and economically. The fear of the museum losing the art proved more urgent to the moneyed elites than the fear of pen-sioners starving. As the museum's chief operating officer smugly declared, "This institution lifts the city above being just another impoverished city." As a result, Orr secured $466 million in pledges, primarily from private foundations, and $350 million in long-term state funding to pay off the pensioners in exchange for protecting the art.[30]

After much anguish and turmoil, the pensioners took the settlement. It was a sign of how much they had struggled and how far they had come from Orr's initial 10 percent offer. But it could not be savored as a true victory. Those figures still amounted to cuts to pensions they believed were protected by the state constitution and had planned their lives around. Moreover, the pension givebacks came on top of other major cuts. The end of cost-of-living allowances means that the real value of pensions will decline with inflation. Furthermore, Orr brought an end to city-sponsored health-care coverage for nearly 20,000 retirees and managed to gut the value of their health-care benefits by 90 percent. In fact, Orr calculated that long-term health-care obligations to the pensioners were far more burdensome to the city than the pensions themselves. Central to Orr's strategy was that Obamacare would make up some of the difference in coverage that was lost. However, even that inadequate formulation could now fall apart with the GOP promising to repeal Obamacare.[31]

In the end, the pension settlements created another two-tiered system, reminiscent of the auto industry, and firmly established the neoliberal restructuring Orr and Snyder sought. The retirees could keep much of their pensions, so long as they allowed "givebacks" and relinquished benefits they had previously won in collective bargaining. Furthermore, Orr essentially made sure that this group of "legacy" workers would be the last of their kind.

Once the pensioners settled, they broke the coalition of convenience with the Wall Street creditors Syncora and FGIC.

Settling for only 13 cents on the dollar, the latter were the biggest losers on paper; nevertheless, there was a big silver lining for them. Both received access to Downtown Detroit land and property rights that could prove to be far more valuable in the future. Whether one thought Detroit got the best of the deal or not, the city was sure to have a bevy of financiers exerting a greater impact on its development and its future.[32]

CHANGE YOU CAN BANK ON

When all the negotiations were finalized, Orr boasted that the emergency manager's plan of adjustment to settle the bankruptcy would free up $1.7 billion for what the plan's disclosure statement called "meaningful and necessary investment" over the next decade to improve city services, foster economic and residential growth, reduce crime, and remove blight. Yet the plan of adjustment disclosed a caveat that the projections were not prepared in compliance with federal or professional standards of accounting and that the city could not be held to them in the future.[33]

Indeed, Detroiters had multiple reasons to be skeptical of the promises advertised in the plan of adjustment. Only about one-half of the $1.7 billion dedicated was the result of savings from debt reduction, representing the aspects of the plan that were most settled by the bankruptcy. The other half was projected by Orr to come from increased revenues and reduced expenses in future years, based on the restructuring of city governance, operation, and services. While some of the projected $358 million in reduced expenses was attributed to increased efficiency, a significant portion would be achieved through privatization measures that would undermine unions and channel much of the city's business to companies and workers outside of the city.

In particular, Orr sold the city's trash collection to Rizzo Environmental Services and Advanced Disposal—a company that unraveled in 2016 when an FBI probe revealed evidence it had bribed public officials. Perhaps most disconcerting with regard to potential conflicts of interest was Orr's talk of privatizing and outsourcing aspects of planning and development.[34]

Orr's projected $483 million increase in revenues over 10 years also sounded like a great boon for the city. The downside, however, is that the projection is based on increasing fees, fines, and burdens on the people of Detroit for daily necessities like buses and parking. The most controversial attempt to reduce costs and increase revenues was the order to shut off running water to residents with unpaid bills from the Detroit Water and Sewer Department (DWSD). Starting in March 2014, this resulted in 3,000 households being cut off from service each week. At a time when corporate and industrial accounts—including the Detroit Red Wings hockey team, Ford Field, and the private contractor of city golf courses—owed $30 million to DWSD, the shutoffs targeted the most vulnerable low-income and household users.[35]

Orr first threatened to sell the city's water operations or even its entire water system to Veolia, the world's largest private water corporation with 728 operations in 66 countries as of December 2009. In an age of rising freshwater scarcity, the idea of privatizing such a precious resource essential to life was bone chilling to many Detroiters. Although Orr backed away from this plan, the threat of privatization spurred support for taking the water department out of the hands of Detroit and placing it under a regional authority that would give the suburbs their long-desired control of operations.[36]

Regardless of the plan of adjustment's soundness, there is no alternative to it for Detroit under current law. Before the emergency manager left office, the state created the Michigan Financial Review Commission to ensure that Detroit's city government would be subject to the dictates of the emergency management regime for at least 13 years. The new law grants the governor the power to appoint most of the commission's members and binds elected officials to seek the commission's seal of approval for a vast array of central activities and operations. Specifically, the law requires the city to have its budgets, financial plans, contracts, and collective-bargaining agreements approved by the commission. The city must also appoint a chief financial officer that the commission approves. In order for the city to be released from oversight, it must first achieve "deficit-free budgets for 3 consecutive years," then demonstrate to the commission that it is complying with both the plan for adjustment and the law's mandates for "10 consecutive fiscal years." This is receivership continued by other means.[37]

When Kevyn Orr issued his final report as emergency manager and resigned his position, he asserted that his regime marked "an historic turning point for the City." Orr proclaimed, "Detroit now has an opportunity to chip away at decades of financial mismanagement and to return this iconic town to its rightful place among great American cities." The cause for hope, he argued, came particularly from the "reinvestment initiatives" built into the plan of adjustment. The largest sum of $460 million was set aside for tackling an estimated 78,000 blighted and abandoned structures. A close second in priority spending was public safety, for which Orr dedicated $430 million, with roughly two-thirds of that devoted to policing. Though acknowledging it "appeared inflated," Orr repeated the widely circulated claim that Detroit had an average 58-minute police response time "for top priority emergencies." He further stressed that the "murder rate" was "highest in the nation and more than ten times the national average."[38]

Even if we accept Orr's most optimistic financial projections, one must still wonder about the social viability of a plan designed by a corporate lawyer who was guided by financial consultants and deliberately removed from interaction with actual city residents. Detroit's privatization of core city services is part of a worrisome nationwide trend that has dramatically escalated, since the 2008 recession, in municipalities small and large and in urban and rural areas. In a series of reports launched in 2016, the *New York Times* found that private equity firms in pursuit of returns on investment have—not surprisingly—jacked up rates after taking over public water systems. Private control of public matters of life and death, however, extends far deeper. "When you dial 911," read one headline, "Wall Street answers." For-profit management of emergency care and firefighting has often produced "dire results," including inhumane cost cutting and localities left with an ambulance shortage when companies go belly up. Public officials rushing headlong into neoliberal privatization are literally playing with fire.[39]

Although Orr claimed to have learned from history, nowhere in his plan does he acknowledge that "blight removal" and policing have been the source of more controversy than arguably any other issues in the modern history of Detroit city governance. The issue has not been a lack of money for these concerns: it is that the hundreds of millions spent on "urban renewal" and "public safety" have intensified racism and inequality.

During the 1940s, the wholesale demolition of the Detroit's Black Bottom neighborhood displaced the largest concentration of African American residents before World War II. Carried out in the name of "slum removal" and false promises of "improvement," it remains to this day a cautionary tale at the forefront of black consciousness in in the city. Indeed, Orr gave Detroiters more than ample cause to fear the impact of his so-called improvements. On the issue of "blight removal," the stated goal is to "raise investor confidence and effect lasting change in economic growth and quality of life."[40]

Orr's definition of "quality of life" also came under question when he took a brazen step on policing. He paid $590,000 to hire the Manhattan Institute and the Bratton Group as consultants to implement "stop and frisk" policing procedures in Detroit shortly after they were declared unconstitutional in New York. In an ominous sign of the growing counter-revolution, Detroit infamously became the place of safe harbor for a practice that had been cast off elsewhere as ineffective, discriminatory, and illegal. Detroit would not, however, identify as a "sanctuary city," as many others did in response to Trump's election. Echoing the mayor's office, Police Chief James Craig, who had been installed by the emergency manager, insisted that local authorities would share information and assist the federal government with deporting undocumented immigrants. These developments symbolized a neoliberal restructuring process that sought to impose discipline on poor and working-class residents to satisfy right-wing politicians and Wall Street financiers.[41]

FOUR

Race to the Bottom

"Can I shoot someone in a hoodie?"[1]

Jim Bonsall, Detroit's chief financial officer under Kevyn Orr, shocked and offended his primarily black coworkers with this callous swipe belittling the death of Trayvon Martin. The flippant quip from Bonsall, a 60-year-old white man, derailed a sober conversation about the annual Angel's Night neighborhood patrols designed to curtail arson during Halloween. It was a telling but terminal act of arrogance from a corporate "turnaround" specialist, who built his reputation as a self-described "pit bull." Buoyed by friends with connections to the governor, Bonsall had entered the position vowing to take harsh measures to maximize revenue while applying new metrics to crack down on subordinate workers he felt were apathetic and made too many excuses.[2]

Cheryl Johnson, Detroit's treasurer and a black woman, filed a formal complaint accusing Bonsall of misconduct, abuse, and fostering a hostile work environment, especially for African American employees. Despite issuing a public apology, saying "It was never my intention to offend anyone," Bonsall was chastised by Governor Rick Snyder and Mayor Mike Duggan, and Emergency Manager Orr pushed him to resign. His problem, however, stemmed less from his cavalier attitude about black lives and more from his inability to keep his comments private. Bonsall's job was to administer devastating austerity measures, which the state takeover had facilitated by taking a sledgehammer to two interrelated pillars of the black freedom struggle: the sanctity of the right to vote, which civil rights activists fought and died for; and the right to "community control," which embodied the Black Power movement's call for self-determination. He got into trouble when he removed the fig leaf of tolerance that allowed the architects of neoliberal restructuring to claim they were "post-racial" in their orientation.[3]

This chapter begins by exploring the depths to which the discourse of race sank during the bankruptcy, as Orr and Duggan reduced ideas of racial diversity and equity to tokenism or worse. By ignoring all of the structural forces behind Detroit's crisis, Orr and Duggan could assert that black political power had failed in ways that necessitated putting the city in the hands of an unelected emergency manager and a white mayor. However, evidence from the long-term rule of Detroit Public Schools by emergency managers demonstrates that neoliberal restructuring and "school choice" policies have only made things worse.

THE NEW POLARIZATION

One of the paradoxes of recent history is that we have witnessed some of the worst outbreaks of racist violence and injustice at the very moment when African Americans and other people of color have finally ascended to the White House and other high-ranking offices within U.S. society. The great sense of hope that propelled millions of people, especially African Americans, to campaign for Barack Obama in 2008 faded as the rash of indiscriminate police killings of African Americans produced an overwhelming sense of sorrow and outrage. The rise of white nationalism tied to Donald Trump's election further created a renewed sense of racial division and terror.

The "whitelash" against Obama at the scale of the nation, based not on assessment of his positions but on a delegitimation of his presidency and personhood, recalls the impact of Coleman Young's election on race and politics in metropolitan Detroit. Although black Detroiters have often expressed profound disappointment in the performance in their elected officials, many have also felt a sense of pride that they live in a city governed by African Americans. It is a sign of the rebellion's ongoing legacy that whites have found this difficult to swallow. Most of the college students whom I taught at the University of Michigan during Obama's first term—primarily whites from the suburbs surrounding Detroit—could not fathom placing the foul-mouthed and street-smart Young in the same category as the Harvard-educated president. Obama was, in many of their eyes, a transcendent figure ready to promote reconciliation. No matter how moderate his policies or appearance, however, the counter-revolution branded Obama an extremist, anti-white, and hostile to business in many of the same ways it had done to Young.

The parallel has also provided a crucial lesson for African Americans and social justice advocates. Elected officials, even the most talented and gifted ones, are ultimately a product of the system in which they are produced. They may do things in office that are quite consequential, such as when Young desegregated the police department; however, these acts do not fundamentally alter the structures and attitudes that have become embedded within the city or nation over many decades. That is why activists assert that social change requires protracted organizing and consciousness-raising at all levels of society.

Fifty years ago, the Black Power movement raised structural demands, many of which emanated directly from the lives and concerns of working-class people, while also expressing a fundamental belief that the white power structure must give way to black "community control." As the Shrine of the Black Madonna's Reverend Cleage once stated, whites needed to "stop trying to live in the suburbs and run our black community." The persistence of social ills and lack of structural transformation has ultimately exposed the limited value of "black faces in high places." African American studies scholar Keeanga-Yamahtta Taylor has criticized the "cloak of imagined racial solidarity" that black politicians have used to ignore "their role as arbiters of political power who willingly operate in a political terrain designed to exploit and oppress African Americans and other working-class people."[4]

While voters in Detroit overwhelmingly identify as Democrats, the city's politics reflect the intra-party between Democratic politicians who answer primarily to working-class residents and those who cater to the corporate elite. This fissure reflects the class polarization within communities of color that has been a central feature of neoliberalism. In the aftermath of the civil rights movement, stereotypes and modes of oppression against African Americans have been focused especially on those who are working-class, structurally unemployed, or stigmatized as members of the "underclass." At the same time, corporations in the age of globalized capitalism have come to prize diversity and multiculturalism. While they are not interested in ending structural poverty, corporate employers are deeply committed to

mining communities of color for their most talented and edu-
cated members and to developing profit-making strategies
informed by racial knowledge. The same forces giving rise to a
new class of elites of color have simultaneously undermined the
economic standing of working-class communities of color.

THE NEOLIBERAL FRATERNITY

Detroit's bankruptcy pushed the politics of "imagined racial solidarity" to farcical levels. As the system has come to rely on black
actors to carry out its dirty work, black political representation
has been reduced to caricature. For the architects of neoliberal
restructuring, it was an imperative that the public face of their
project be black, and they have been up-front in acknowledging
this. Investment banker Kenneth Buckfire, who pushed the Snyder administration to pursue a Detroit bankruptcy at least as
early as December 2010, served as the primary financial advisor
to the emergency management regime. "We strongly believed
that the emergency manager should be an African American,"
Buckfire told reporter Nathan Bomey. "Clearly given the political tensions and history of race relations in the city, if the emergency manager was a white person, and even if they were the
most qualified candidate, people would characterize the choice
as, 'Whitey's taking over the city again.'"[5]

Playing up Orr's blackness became a key tactic to counter the
concern that appointing an emergency manager would look—in
the words of a senior Jones Day lawyer—like "a fascist takeover." Snyder's publicity team worked overtime to present Orr as
a Democrat and a product of the black community—a son of
civil rights activists who was raised in the South, his father an
African Methodist Episcopal preacher. Returning the favor, Orr

stated, according to *MLive.com,* that Snyder's actions to push for Detroit's bankruptcy demonstrated "political courage on par with Gen. Dwight D. Eisenhower's D-Day Invasion and the Rev. Martin Luther King's civil rights crusade."[6]

From Snyder on down, the white men who engineered the state takeover cast themselves as Detroit's saviors. Noting that he is the grandchild of refugees who fled Europe, Buckfire asserted that he felt a calling "to help restructure Detroit" and that this work aligned with "an old Jewish principle that you ought to make the world better every day." In fact, Buckfire's desire to do good deeds coincided with his firm, Miller Buckfire, taking in a $22.82 million payday. Kevyn Orr returned to work at the law firm Jones Day, which was $57.9 million richer after being paid by Detroit. David Heiman, a partner with Jones Day, charged $1,075 an hour. He also routinely billed the city for his lavish travel costs and meals plus roughly $500 an hour for all his nonworking time spent traveling. The types of high-rolling expenses on the public dime that led the media and public to brand Kwame Kilpatrick a criminal became routine under emergency management.[7]

Conway MacKenzie raked in $17.28 million in fees for consulting on "operational restructuring." The firm recommended not only that the city council shed over two-thirds of its staff but also that the council members themselves be reduced to part-time employees. In other words, private consultants, brought in against the will of Detroit's citizens, arranged a plan that would reduce the role of elected officials and people's access to their representatives.[8]

Consultants from the likes of Conway MacKenzie preached austerity for the city while exuding extravagance. They billed the city $275 an hour for the work of a 22-year-old entry-level staffer fresh out of college. In 2012, the same consulting firm had thrown itself a decadent $1.5 million party, where models were paid to serve 450 carafes of Dom Perignon to guests that included Mike Tyson. Furthermore, it capitalized on its CEO's longtime friendship with Snyder's state treasurer, Andy Dillon, to secure its role in the emergency management regime. After Dillon was pressured to resign under an ethical cloud of controversy in fall 2013, he took a high-paying job with the consulting firm.[9]

In total, lawyers and consultants racked up over $170 million in fees from the bankruptcy. The *Detroit News* called it "the most expensive municipal restructuring in U.S. history." Judge Rhodes, however, did not bat an eyelid before approving the massive payout. Indeed, he declared that the people of Detroit should "feel and express a strong and genuine sense of appreciation for these professionals and their service." Shortly after, Judge Rhodes joined Dillon on Conway MacKenzie's payroll, both working as private consultants on Puerto Rico's debt crisis. Fortunately for the city, the judge commissioned an overseer, Robert Fishman, to monitor expenses by private contractors. Unfortunately, Fishman also charged Detroit $618 an hour, which he considered a "discount off his usual rate of $695." The city's bill to guard against excessive spending ultimately surpassed $1 million. On top of this, Jones Day billed the city tens of thousands of dollars in additional expenses for the time it spent going over its fees with the examiner.[10]

All around, the lawyers and consultants patted themselves on the back for a job well done. It was a consistent theme that the private-sector professionals gave the city their services at a discount—even though it only resulted from a complaint by the city. The prevalence of this narrative proved how much the lawyers and consultants had succeeded in normalizing their reign over city hall. The University of Michigan Law School served as the glue binding together the neoliberal fraternity members, including Orr, Snyder, Rhodes, and Duggan. We can add to the list Michael McGee, the CEO of Miller Canfield, which received the fifth-highest bankruptcy payout at nearly $7 million in fees. McGee's law firm reported that he "played a major role in the drafting of Michigan's emergency management law."[11]

Limited to a $275,000 annual salary, Orr was portrayed as the most self-sacrificing of all. He seemed to blend in effortlessly, as if he were the only black member of an all-white fraternity, and his loyalty did not go unrewarded. After Orr was appointed emergency manager, investigative reporters found that he had liens on his home because he had failed to uphold his obligation to pay thousands of dollars in payroll taxes. Governor Snyder conveniently disregarded the fact that Orr had committed exactly the sort of legally and financially negligent acts that Detroiters were being individually and collectively punished for.[12]

The fraternity culture involved more than ill-advised locker-room talk about shooting young men in hoodies. It was a reflection of a patriarchal order in which a small cabal of wealthy men were given top-down authority to make decisions that would impact hundreds of thousands of lives. The bankruptcy served as a high-stakes competition reducing those lives to numbers on a spreadsheet. Orr slipped casually into misogynistic and homophobic language to describe his testosterone-laden dustups with other lawyers. On the record, Orr described his response to a confrontational move by opposing counsel as "We ain't gonna be your bitch."[13]

In fact, Orr's white superiors were often more concerned about appearances than he was. Stirring controversy in one of his first major interviews after taking office, Orr stated that he understood people viewed him as a "dictator" but that he would be a "benevolent" one. He then insulted Detroiters by saying that "for too long the city was dumb, lazy, happy and rich."[14] Orr's racial performance was most outlandish but also most successful in front of predominantly white audiences. In November 2013, he affected an excited and militant tone before the University of Michigan Law School while claiming that he entered college as a revolutionary socialist determined to tear down the system. He also stated that taking on the emergency manager position meant putting aside an "affluent career," with a sports car, a beach home in Miami, and a "hot blonde" mistress.[15]

Sadly, Orr's contrived act seemed pitch perfect for the audience of aspiring lawyers. He played up and reinforced crude stereotypes of black masculinity, deploying them as stand-ins for African American politicians, workers, and voters in Detroit. He offered his own trajectory toward becoming a fiscally responsible and morally upright public servant as an analogy for his quest to correct what he and his audience understood to be Detroit's fiscal and moral failings. He later stated that his "number one concern" when taking the emergency manager post was "civil unrest." It was yet another way to identify with the suburban mindset, still guided by fear five decades after the 1967 rebellion.

Literally looking down on Detroit from a penthouse suite, Orr took up residence in the historic Westin Book Cadillac, a luxury hotel-condo that was another symbol of the two-tiered society. After being shuttered and stripped for two decades, the Book Cadillac reopened in 2008, following a $180 million renovation made possible by a creative mix of private financing, tax credits, and public subsidies. Hailed as a game-changing development for Downtown and the city's convention business, its revival was celebrated by architecture critics and preservationists. When Orr moved in, however, the hotel was far from profit-able. In fact, its owner, the Ferchill Group, was skipping its pay-ments on over $3 million in loans the city had arranged through HUD, contributing to a total of $24 million in delinquent city-approved loans, mainly for luxury hotel and loft developments. As journalist Stephen Henderson reported, these delinquencies cost the city $7 million a year in federal block-grant funds that most residents would have expected to be devoted to affordable housing and low-income community development.[16]

What's more, the hotel's owners had failed to make a single principal or interest payment on another $24 million it had bor-rowed from Detroit's two municipal pension funds. Incredibly, while excoriating the city and pension-fund trustees for finan-cial irresponsibility and mismanagement, Orr did nothing mate-rially or even symbolically to hold accountable the owners of the opulent hotel he was living in. A legal settlement with the hotel in 2016 left the pension funds with no accrued interest and a 50 percent loss on their principal.[17]

Orr's representation of himself as the perfect embodiment of the "post-racial" establishment paved the way for his trumpet-ing the fall 2013 election of Mike Duggan as mayor of Detroit. Duggan was yet another white male figure known as a "turna-round" expert ready to make the city more "business-friendly." A product of Democratic machine politics in Wayne County under Edward McNamara, he left government in 2004 to work as CEO of the Detroit Medical Center (DMC), the region's largest network of hospitals and clinics. Starting with a boost of bailout money from the state, Duggan steered a restructuring process that led to the nonprofit DMC being sold to venture capitalists through a 2010 deal spurred by public subsidies. "The nonprofit model is killing health care in the city of Detroit," he stated, while insisting the DMC needed an infusion of capital that could only come from Wall Street.[18]

Two years after brokering the DMC sale, Duggan resigned as CEO and relocated from the suburbs to run for mayor. Calling Duggan "the first white mayor … in the past fifty-some odd years" (the actual figure was 40), Orr told the law students this was a sign that "people are moving beyond the old ways." He implored them to "forget race, forget class" and focus on "who's gonna do the job?" Orr was mouthing the fallacious conservative argument that diversity, equity, and affirmative action are at odds with the pursuit of competency and excellence. Even in Ann Arbor, these words would probably have been deemed racist if they came out of the mouth of a white man. Orr, however, was granting the young professionals a license to overlook their own race and class privilege; he encouraged these "post-racial" millennials to envision themselves saving Detroit just as he believed he was doing.[19]

For his part, Duggan campaigned for mayor in 2013 saying that Obama was his role model because he transcended race. After winning the primary, he declared, "People want change. They don't see color." His election was undoubtedly a sign of changing political conditions within the city. Indeed, many black Detroiters were so frustrated with the black political class, they were willing to give a shot to an outsider like Duggan. My own sense, however, is that the state takeover, coming in the wake of the 2008–09 Kilpatrick scandal, demoralized many residents. Voter turnout was only 25 percent, falling in absolute numbers from 235,000 in 2005 to 135,000 in 2013.[20] And among those going to the polls, the election seemed to boil down to a dubious proposition: Would you rather have a white mayor or continue with a black emergency manager?

In contrast to his scathing criticism of Detroit's former mayors, Orr had nothing but praise to offer Duggan. For mainstream media and political observers, Duggan's election was an opportunity to reboot Detroit governance: a do-over of the period before the 1967 rebellion when a white Democrat was mayor and black elites played a supporting role. (Officially, Detroit municipal elections are nonpartisan, but Duggan's connection to the Democratic Party is well known.) Like Orr, Duggan has also received generally favorable national media coverage, even though there are sufficient questions about current and past practices in office to brand him as just another "corrupt" politician. Despite an ongoing federal investigation into mishandling of funds and contracts for demolitions, the mayor has retained good favorability ratings, in part by managing expectations.[21]

The reality is that the mayor's agenda is heavily defined by the parameters of the corporate restructuring plan. Can such a plan work in a city with a high percentage of residents in poverty? Doubts have certainly been sown, now that the halo over Duggan's "turnaround" of the DMC has faded. Not only is the DMC's long-term commitment to subsidizing low-income patients uncertain under corporate ownership; recently, it has also been the subject of a major scandal for its long-standing failure to properly sterilize surgical equipment, dating back to Duggan's time as CEO.[22]

FALSE CHOICES IN SCHOOL REFORM

During the 20th century, Detroit's schools were at the center of heated conflicts over racial segregation and inequality. Over the past decades, however, the right wing has targeted the survival of the public school system itself. Fueled by wealthy donors and foundations, the charge has been led, in particular, by a wealthy couple based in western Michigan exerting outsized influence over the state's Republican Party: Betsy DeVos, Trump's secretary of education, and Dick DeVos, the billionaire heir to the Amway fortune and 2006 GOP candidate for governor.

Right-wing "school choice" reformers like Betsy DeVos foresee the actual or effective elimination of the Detroit Public Schools (DPS) system. Viewing neoliberal education as the key to "advance God's kingdom," DeVos and other key funders of the political push for Michigan's first charter-school law in 1993 came from a right-wing, Christian orientation. They saw charter schools as an interim political step toward the establishment of vouchers for parochial schools and made common cause with the GOP's libertarian wing in seeking to privatize education. In February 2016, DeVos called for ending DPS, arguing this would "liberate" students from the "district model" of education by creating "a system of schools where performance and competition create high-quality opportunities for kids."[23]

Ever since Governor John Engler, a Republican, ordered a state takeover in 1999, a separate process of emergency management has run DPS. This long-range experiment has been an unmitigated disaster, a means to avoid addressing the problem of structural inequity while forcing privatization and neoliberal measures on families, teachers, and board members. Although Engler declared that the district suffered from mismanagement and low academic achievement, DPS entered emergency management with a $100 million surplus that became a $500 million deficit by 2016. Critics suspected that the political motive behind the state takeover was control of voter-approved school-renovation bond funds initially worth $1.5 billion. After a brief restoration of local governance, the resumption of DPS emergency management under Governor Jennifer Granholm, a Democrat, proved no better. Still more state-appointed leaders were brought in after Rick Snyder became governor, including Jack Martin, whose negligence led to a complete loss of federal Head Start funding in 2014. The following year, Snyder recycled Flint's former emergency manager, Darnell Earley, to run DPS after he had overseen Flint's nightmarish switch to polluted water. In 2016, Snyder turned to Judge Rhodes, who had retired from the bench after settling Detroit's bankruptcy, and Rhodes accepted the job despite admitting he lacked any experience in education.[24]

The crisis of DPS is evident in its rapid enrollment decline. In 2000, DPS had 162,693 students. While this was a far cry from its peak enrollment of nearly 300,000 in 1966, the numbers had stabilized and even grown during the 1990s. The first state takeover, however, produced an immediate loss of over 5,000 students and $71.4 million in state funding, causing major disruptions that made both academic and financial planning extremely difficult to carry out under duress and uncertainty. School closures designed to save money hastened a downward spiral. While some buildings were sold, many were abandoned and became a new liability on both DPS and the neighborhoods they once anchored. From 2000 to 2015, DPS closed a jaw-dropping 195 schools, leaving only 93 remaining. The pace of closures exhausted students; some were forced to transfer schools on what seemed like a yearly basis. Moreover, new enrollment boundaries caused heightened stress and social tension by cavalierly throwing together students from neighborhoods with intense gang rivalries. By 2015, DPS was down to only 47,959 students. Many of the remaining schools harbor decrepit conditions that have been exposed to the public by teachers posting photos to Twitter in protest.[25]

The imperative to shutter buildings and slash budgets left no space for some renowned DPS schools like the Catherine

Ferguson Academy (CFA) to survive. Under the leadership of Principal Asenath Andrews, CFA established a supportive and nurturing environment for teenage mothers and pregnant girls. Founded in 1985, it was initially based in a Salvation Army building and operated what Andrews critiqued as a "warehouse-segregation model," teaching little more than basic domestic and vocational skills. Andrews had the audacity to believe that the school could develop a successful college-prep curriculum if it was sensitive not only to the academic but also to the material and emotional needs of its students. Moving into its own building on the near Westside, CFA created an on-site child-care center and a working farm with fruits, vegetables, and even livestock. The school and farm stood out amid a devastated neighborhood where abandoned factories left toxic scars on a landscape covered with more vacant lots than inhabited homes.[26]

The practical learning model had a profound effect on the young mothers, who learned about lactation while milking goats and physics by building a barn. Most of all, they developed a sense of self-worth and self-confidence that was instantly recognizable to their families, teachers, and observers. Graduation rates reflected undeniable success. Nationwide, only 40 percent of women of all races who have a baby before age 18 finish high school. At CFA, a stunning 95 percent of students completed their degree, well above Detroit's 62 percent average rate. Moreover, as part of the school's program, all graduates achieved acceptance to college. After the emergency financial manager took over DPS in 2009, however, CFA was marked for closure because of its higher-than-average operating cost. An outpouring of student advocacy and public support temporarily spared CFA. Nevertheless, after spending its final few years as a charter school, its closure in 2014 added to a growing list of sorrow stories.[27]

Within 15 years, DPS had lost 70 percent of its student enroll-ment. Where did all those students go? The obvious long-standing concerns were students dropping out and becoming part of the school-to-prison pipeline. During the 1990s, several new factors permanently altered the structural conditions of public education in Detroit. In 1993–94, amid conservative demands to lower taxes, the state legislature eliminated all property taxes devoted to schools. Under a new formula called Proposal A, education funding was centralized with the promise of equalizing allocations across districts. By tying funding to enrollment, however, the state set up a new scenario whereby schools and districts would now compete for students. Spurred by proponents of "school choice," Michigan adopted new meas-ures that allowed school districts to enroll students from outside their boundaries and established some of the nation's most per-missive policies for opening charter schools.[28]

While some celebrated the end of the public school "monop-oly," others saw a recipe for chaos. Although wealthy districts like Grosse Pointe adamantly refused attendance by Detroit residents, a number of inner-ring suburbs that had become inte-grated or even majority black began recruiting Detroit students. Some Detroit families fully relocated to the suburbs. Others continued to live in Detroit but enrolled their children outside the city. Charters had an even bigger impact on the decline in DPS enrollment. By 2014–15, there were as many or more schools and students within the city's charters as there were in DPS.[29]

While a range of "school choice" measures have attracted lib-eral and conservative support nationally, Michigan's headfirst dive into charter schools has stood out as a radical experiment in deregulation and privatization, at an annual cost of $1 billion in state funding. Through the popularization of ideas promoted

in films like *Waiting for Superman,* the charters' rapid prolifera-
tion is based on the notion that public schools are such a disaster
that any new idea should be tried. Arne Duncan, secretary of
education for the Obama administration, once stated, "I think
the best thing that happened to the education system in New
Orleans was Hurricane Katrina." Duncan repeatedly called
Detroit "Ground Zero for education in this country" and cited
the dismantling of the public school system in New Orleans as
the model for change. Echoing the ideology behind Detroit's
corporate restructuring, many school-choice advocates insist
that reducing the role of government and labor unions will mag-
ically increase efficiency. For-profit companies run approxi-
mately 80 percent of the state's charter schools.[30]

The combination of the profit motive and lack of oversight has
led many schools to focus on cutting costs in order to pocket as
much funding as possible. Michigan charter schools spend an
average of $2,000 less per pupil than traditional public schools.
Many of their hiring and spending decisions have raised alarm
about corruption and mismanagement. Because the financial
concerns of their owners trump the needs of students, some
schools have closed abruptly, while others have lingered on
despite a dreadful lack of success. The schools with the best reputation are oversubscribed. Although by law they are required to
admit students randomly, the selective charter schools have long
and complicated application processes that function as filters.
Furthermore, most charters offer no bus transportation, and they
have taken few steps to promote the inclusion of special education students, the vast majority of whom remain in DPS. Nevertheless, with some notable exceptions, the charters as a whole
have failed to improve academic achievement in a significant
way, even by the warped measure of standardized testing.[31]

School privatization and the rise of the charter school industry reflect the changing relationship of capitalism to K–12 education. During the industrial era, public schooling helped to
reproduce class hierarchy through tracking and socialization. A
small minority of working-class students with exceptional skill,
motivation, and the blessing of teachers and counselors made it
to college and a pathway toward the professional and managerial
class. For most, however, schools provided a rudimentary set of
skills along with the discipline and gendered socialization
expected of factory and service workers. In these ways, students
were a future source of surplus value, and schooling *indirectly*
contributed to the manufacturing and sale of corporate products. By contrast, students in postindustrial Detroit have *become*
the product. The pretext that K–12 schooling is a way station
preceding industrial employment has largely evaporated along
with the factory jobs. Profiteers now look to extract value from
the students themselves. Poor urban children may be lacking in
disposable income, but taken collectively they are now a source
of billions of dollars in public appropriations the private sector
has moved to seize. The most grotesque sign of this occurs on
"count day"—the biannual census used to determine state funding allocations. Charter schools launch marketing blitzes and
host pizza parties where they raffle off iPads, and public schools
have followed suit.[32]

Garnering $45 million from the Broad Foundation and other
school-choice backers in 2011–12, the state's creation of the
Educational Achievement Authority (EAA) has been another
example of a high-risk failure. Citing the shortcomings of DPS,
Snyder moved to place 15 of Detroit's "lowest performing"
schools into a state-run "turnaround district." Freed from the
supposed bureaucracy of DPS, the EAA promised to establish

an innovative curriculum marked by the creative use of computers and technology, with teachers drawn from among the plucky college graduates in Teach for America. Instead, the EAA has become yet another opening to newfangled schemes, privatization, and scandal, with Detroit students served up as the guinea pigs. Even its chancellor admits that the EAA has become a "toxic name," and it will relinquish control of the schools it took from DPS in July 2017.[33]

In 2016, the Republicans running state government determined that DPS was close to insolvent. Unlike the case with the city, they balked on bankruptcy. Most of the debt was borrowed from the state government, which thus stood to be the big loser in bankruptcy. Instead, the GOP legislators came up with a scheme eerily reminiscent of Detroit's pension bond plan. DPS was split into two districts, a shell district that would exist entirely to serve as the home for debt and a new district that would operate the schools and start debt free. The new law implemented strict financial oversight by the state, while loosening academic oversight to make Detroit the only city in Michigan to allow the regular hiring of uncertified teachers. It also introduced regressive antistrike provisions to crack down on the activism of teachers, who had staged a mass sick-out to prevent Rhodes from withholding pay for work they already performed. Although Detroit is projected to have its local school board restored in 2017, critics assert that the "new" school district has been set up to fail. Heightening such fears, Attorney General Bill Schuette, a prospective GOP candidate for governor in 2018, ruled that the state may be required to close 27 more Detroit public schools within a year.[34]

Expunged from the legislation was any measure for the city to regulate charter schools or to form a local commission to manage their over-proliferation in Detroit—which, between DPS and charters, now has a combined 30,000 unfilled spaces for students. Journalist Stephen Henderson has linked the GOP's defense of the charter school industry to massive funding and lobbying efforts by school-choice and privatization proponents. During the months in and around the legislative debate over restructuring DPS, the DeVos family contributed $1.45 million to the Republican Party and individual politicians. While the money was the carrot, the stick was a threat to challenge incumbents in the GOP primary.[35]

With schools characterized by racial segregation and inequity, the "new normal" has reprised the dark underside of the city's golden era. Along the same lines, the emergency manager promised to solve Detroit's problems with more policing, blight removal, and corporate investment. Quite incredibly, it seems that the forces that produced global economic calamity are being used to reinforce the social and political conditions underlying the rebellion of 1967.

FIVE

Government for the 1 Percent

In April 2013, the *New York Times* ran a prominent feature story on billionaire financier and developer Dan Gilbert under the headline "A Missionary's Quest to Remake Motor City." It fed a new trend within the national media touting Gilbert as the city's savior. The lengthy article referring to Downtown Detroit as "strange and a little otherworldly" perfectly embodied the narrative of the city as a blank slate. It described a place filled with "empty, decrepit buildings," where "there is no traffic" even at rush hour. Harking back to images of the city's so-called golden age, it concluded that Gilbert's boosterism was driven by the notion "that you can feel nostalgia for a place you've never actually been."[1] This downtown revival follows a national model of urban development producing a sanitized landscape of manufactured authenticity in which the well-off can walk the streets, patronize retail establishments, and enjoy open-air entertainment under the protective cover of private security and surveillance.

Making the city ultra-friendly to corporate investment was not only a goal of the emergency management regime; it was also deemed the only hope for saving the city. Detroit's central core came to be dominated by two of the richest men in the world. Its reputation as a site of abandonment and decay has been replaced by the promotion of "Detroit 2.0" as a new boomtown. This sense of opportunity has been drawing investors, journalists, artists, entrepreneurs, and activists from all over to Detroit—some to collect stories, others to live, work, and stay. Competing with the existing and widely circulated images of "ruin porn," the new narrative of Detroit's "great comeback story" has traversed the nation and crossed international borders. In September 2016, Canada's most widely read newspaper, the *Toronto Star,* advised tourists to "stop being scared of Detroit." Show Me Detroit Tours founder Kim Rusinow declared, "We're a blank canvas at this point—we have so many opportunities to be creative."[2]

This image of Detroit as a blank canvas or blank slate, however, strikes many longtime residents as a racist dismissal of their history and ongoing presence. Born and raised in the city, artist Bryce Detroit sees it as a new narrative to replace the idea of the city as "so depressed there's nothing there" except for "debris." It gives free reign to "creative, young, white, recent graduates" to claim the city "as if the debris had been cleared." Anthropologist Siobhan Gregory argues that the blank slate narrative builds on the myth of the "frontier" as virgin land and feeds the "White savior" complex.[3] While "Detroit 2.0" is an exciting, new place for some, for others it represents the heightening of old contradictions and the production of novel forms of exclusion.

PUBLIC PARK VS. PRIVATE COMMONWEALTH

In January 2013, the local and national media were buzzing about a new plan to privatize Belle Isle, Frederick Law Olmsted's local version of Central Park perched on an island in the middle of the Detroit River. The plan was the brainchild of Rod Lockwood, a longtime leader of the GOP and chamber of commerce in Michigan, working alongside wealthy and politically well-connected figures. Seeing the city's financial distress as a golden opportunity, they proposed to buy Belle Isle for $1 billion and turn it into a privately owned "city-state," restricted to millionaires and their servants. Belle Isle would severely limit taxation and use its own unit of currency called the "rand." When asked if this was a reference to apartheid, Lockwood replied he had "no idea" the rand was South Africa's currency. He only meant to pay tribute to libertarian Ayn Rand.[4]

The governor and the emergency manager, however, implemented their own agenda for the park. The state government took control of Belle Isle, agreeing to pay for most of its long-overdue renovation and upkeep. The catch was that residents can no longer drive into the park without a state-issued "recreation passport." Control of Belle Isle, where the 1943 riot began, has long been a source of contention. For example, an angry constituent wrote to the mayor: "It seems to be generally accepted that the colored race has completely taken over the City's and State's most beautiful park and playground 'Belle Isle' for which the tax-payers have spent millions of dollars to beautify." Although written seven decades ago, the same sentiments could easily be found in online comments during the debate over the state takeover.[5]

When the city council voted down the state proposal, Orr effectively vetoed their decision and pushed it through. Belle Isle joined the list of the city's most prominent public sites and institutions—including the Detroit Zoo, Detroit Institute of Arts,

Eastern Market, and Cobo Convention Center—still nominally owned by the City of Detroit but controlled by a regional, state, or private nonprofit authority. While proponents of the state's takeover asserted that the $11 fee was not prohibitive, the combination of buying and securing the entry permit provided a new means to restrict access to the park. Critics further asserted that state troopers were aggressively policing traffic and public behavior as a form of racial profiling. In 2014, the state even announced the park would be closed to the public for four days while it was used for a private corporate event. Only after public outcry did it rescind that decision. The new checkpoint to the city's most storied public park has become a symbol of what many either love or hate about the "new" Detroit.[6]

Although the architects of the city-state are still trying to win support for their plan, they have already succeeded in shifting the debate on urban redevelopment. Law professor John Mogk wrote in *Crain's Detroit Business* that their plan was a political nonstarter and "probably unconstitutional." "That said," he argued, "the quest of the wealthy to preserve and expand their wealth should be capitalized upon if it can benefit Detroit." Mogk proposed that "Congress declare Detroit's downtown and Midtown a federal tax-free zone within the city of Detroit. This would give the city all the same benefits without losing Belle Isle."[7]

With the city's bankruptcy serving as the catalyst for a corporate restructuring of Detroit, developers have needed no such federal decree to buy up land and property within the city's most coveted seven-square-mile central core. They have regularly received the support and subsidies they have demanded from local and state government, as well as from existing federal programs.

JOE LOUIS DOESN'T LIVE HERE ANYMORE

At the center of the city's largest ongoing redevelopment project is the family of Mike Ilitch, whose death in February 2017 occurred as his business empire was reaching new heights. He was best known as the founder of Little Caesars Pizza and owner of two of Detroit's professional sports teams, the Tigers and Red Wings. In the 1980s, Ilitch was praised for buying and restoring the historic Fox Theatre as he moved his business headquarters into the midrise building above it. During the '90s, Ilitch expanded his footprint within the Downtown landscape by purchasing the Tigers and moving them to Comerica Park baseball stadium, facing his Fox Theatre. While sandlot purists lamented the demise of old Tiger Stadium, critics also questioned the $85.8 million in public funding Wayne County contributed to build the stadium—a deal that Mike Duggan pushed for as deputy county executive. The amount of the subsidy was slightly more than what Ilitch paid for the team in 1992. (Shortly after, the Detroit Lions' Ford Field was built with $80 million in public subsidies.) To add insult to injury, Comerica Park was named for a bank—formerly Detroit Bank and Trust—that had deliberately dissociated its name from the city in the early '90s and later moved its headquarters to Dallas.[8]

Ilitch and his family had still bigger plans in development. After the new stadium opened in 2000, they stealthily began buying up land, property, and development rights north and west of the Fox Theatre for a new hockey arena. While some of the properties were vacant, in multiple cases they bought up apartment buildings and evicted low-income and disabled tenants. The Ilitches admitted they kept the properties vacant and in states of disrepair in order to depress surrounding property values while they moved to acquire more parcels. The new Little Caesars Arena—announced as a $450 million project that has since ballooned to $627.5 million—is now under construction, with $285 million in public subsidies arranged by the state while Detroit was under bankruptcy. It is the centerpiece of a development project designed to hasten gentrification by connecting Downtown with the rebranded "Midtown" district. The Ilitches were heavy donors to local politicians, and their lobbying efforts have resulted in a wide array of sweetheart deals giving their company free and easy access to land and public dollars. There was no escaping, however, that they pulled their biggest score while city hall was under emergency management, with no effective guardian of the people's interests. The city sold the Ilitches 39 parcels of land for the arena for only one dollar, never bothering to have them appraised.[9]

The lopsided deal may prove to be a bonanza for the Ilitch family. On top of the subsidies, they will get all proceeds from ticket sales, parking, and concessions, as well as the valuable naming rights. The upshot is that Detroit's hockey team will be moving from an arena named for a black Detroit boxing legend to one named for the toga- and sandal-clad, cartoon mascot of a corporate pizza chain. Because the Ilitches will technically lease rather than own the property, they will not pay any property taxes. Incredibly, however, their Red Wings will get free rent on the state-of-the-art arena for up to 95 years. The public paid for demolition and preparation of the construction site, but the Ilitches received city-owned land and control a large swath of the 50-block area marked for redevelopment as the arena district. Thus far, non-Detroiters have received most of the jobs produced. Critics of the arena deal bemoaned the government's failure to secure a robust and legally binding community benefits agreement.[10]

Since the construction of Baltimore's Camden Yards in the '90s, the story driving the nationwide boom in publicly subsidized urban sports arenas and stadiums has been that their construction generates increased retail business and raises property values to offset the subsidies they receive. One projection is that Detroit's hockey arena will create 440 permanent jobs—which, even if true, comes at a steep price. While academic studies have questioned the extent of these economic benefits, the fine print on the hockey arena raises even more concerns. The arena and surrounding development will exist in a special economic zone, allowing the Downtown Development Authority to divert taxes from the state School Aid Fund to the arena (the legislature then has to find a way to repay the education fund). Furthermore, any future increase in taxes from rising property values would go back to the development authority rather than the city. As if that were not enough, Dan Gilbert has tried to push a new bill through the state legislature to aid his proposed soccer-stadium plan by allowing big-time developers to retain not just property taxes but also all retail and income taxes from businesses and residents inside such special zones.[11]

CASS CORRIDOR MEETS "MIDTOWN"

The repeated demand for political intervention belies any claim that developers (or Wall Street bankers) are making their fortunes within a "free" market. Ilitch acquired much of his land in the proposed arena district on the cheap because it had been artificially depressed. It falls within the southern section of the Cass Corridor neighborhood, known for its countercultural history and bounded on the densely settled north by Wayne State University. The city effectively declared this area Detroit's Skid

Row, concentrating homeless populations and soup kitchens in the area. It was also the designated neighborhood of last resort for sex workers and marginalized populations. When the old Chinatown was bulldozed for the postwar construction of the Lodge Freeway, merchants attempted to reestablish a new Chinatown in the lower Cass Corridor but achieved only partial and fleeting success. With the announcement of the arena development, young professionals and entrepreneurs have moved in as property values skyrocket.

One way to discern between old and new residents is whether they call the district the Cass Corridor or "Midtown." A half-century ago, the corridor was the home of hippies, the radical White Panther Party, and poets like John Sinclair, whose 10-year prison sentence for marijuana made him the subject of a global movement—John Lennon, Yoko Ono, and Stevie Wonder rallied to the cause. It was the birthplace of the best kind of "only in Detroit" stories and where Mexican American singer-songwriter Sixto Rodriguez toiled for years before realizing he was internationally famous and becoming the subject of the Academy Award–winning film *Searching for Sugar Man* (2012).[12]

The rebranding of "Midtown" first emanated from a nonprofit-driven "arts, meds, and eds" strategy that positioned museums, hospitals, and university campuses as anchors of a postindustrial economy. Increasingly, these large institutions have been surrounded by residential and retail projects such as lofts, luxury apartments, bed-and-breakfasts, bars, and restaurants, catering to the urban professionals that consultant Richard Florida has dubbed the "creative class." In the age of neoliberalism, urban redevelopment nationwide has increasingly focused on this form of gentrification as a growth strategy. This was the impetus for the city's amassing $5.8 million in public subsidies and private grants to woo Whole Foods to "Midtown" with a new building and rent at one-third market rate. George Jackson, president of the Detroit Economic Growth Corporation, openly declared that his goal was advancing "gentrification." Not long after, he left to form a private consulting firm with the Ilitch family as a main patron.[13]

Whether the neighborhood is better or worse off as a result of these changes is in the eye of the beholder. What has been overshadowed and threatened is the grassroots form of entrepreneurialism that had taken root in the Cass Corridor. In the '90s, the Avalon Bakery was founded by two women, Ann Perrault and Jackie Victor, who were inspired by the late James Boggs's radical vision of building a people-centered local economy out of the ashes of deindustrialization. "In every neighborhood," Boggs stated, "there should be a bakery where families can purchase freshly baked bread and children can stop by after school to buy their sweets."[14] Avalon's owners had deep roots in the city's social justice networks, but admittedly no baking or business experience. They had to humbly acquire these skills and asked for their supporters and customers to be patient as they learned.

Sixteen years ago, activists from the youth leadership organization Detroit Summer founded Back Alley Bikes on Cass Avenue. The simple idea was that low-income youth and adult residents lacking transportation could learn how to build and maintain bikes assembled from used parts and donated bikes. The broader goal was to develop a sense of DIY self-confidence in a city abandoned by the auto industry, as well as a collective sense of mutuality in a nation governed by private enterprise. In recent years, however, "Midtown" has become, for many (especially the national media), synonymous with trendy upstarts like Shinola, which sells $3,000 bikes stamped "Built in Detroit." Founded by the former Fossil chairman, Tom Kartsotis, Shinola was first known for producing watches. However, it has branched out to sell multiple products because its core commodity is actually "manufactured authenticity." In April 2016, Stacy Perman described the company's strategy in *Inc.* magazine: "Virtually everything about Detroit—the locals, the factory, its workers—would become a prop in service of the Shinola brand."[15]

Because so much of the nation has consumed little about Detroit beyond stereotypes, the narratives of corporations like Shinola have not just spread like wildfire, they have done so by seizing the mantle of the "underdog" from the city's longtime residents. Kartsotis has peddled the myth that he set up Shinola in "a rough part of town."[16] In fact, it is located in one of the most walkable centers of the city—a few blocks from a major university and adjacent to the Avalon Bakery, which has been a hub of activity for nearly two decades. This is the "rough part" of Detroit only for those who think gated communities are the norm.

WELCOME TO GILBERTVILLE

Despite the hype surrounding Shinola and the payoff on Ilitch's years of economic and political investments, the architects and players of the "new" Detroit have all been spectacularly upstaged by billionaire Dan Gilbert, whom we met at the beginning of this chapter. Gilbert owns the online mortgage company Quicken Loans plus his real estate wing, Bedrock Detroit. Like many whites of his generation, the 55-year-old Gilbert was born in the city but relocated to the suburbs at an early age. Gilbert has dubbed his project "Detroit 2.0" and has emphasized attracting Silicon Valley–styled capital, entrepreneurs, and high-tech workers. Lured by $50 million in public subsidies, he moved his

Quicken Loans headquarters to Detroit in 2010. With an urban renewal approach he has dubbed "the big bang," Gilbert soon began acquiring Downtown properties, and the impact has been unmistakable. By 2016, he owned 73 properties and controlled at least five others. He had spent $2.2 billion on acquisition and renovation, though he obtained some properties from the city essentially at no cost. "I think we are just starting," Gilbert said. What may look like loose spending was a strategy to capitalize on the financial crisis.[17]

"Wish you bought gold in '06? You'll wish you bought Detroit in '12," declared Gilbert's business partner, venture capitalist John Linkner, in *Forbes* magazine. "Detroit has bottomed out, so now, there's nothing but upside." And in fact, the majority of the Downtown buildings that were vacant when Gilbert arrived are now occupied or have renovation plans. Apartment rents shot up 60 percent over five years, while commercial rents tripled. In May 2015, the headline for a "big story" from the Associated Press blared, "Whites Moving to Detroit, City That Epitomized White Flight."[18]

One of the highest-profile developments mimicking a sanitized theme park design is the QLine streetcar, which was known as the M-1 rail line until Gilbert bought the naming rights. Gilbert, Ilitch, and other corporate moguls such as Roger Penske recruited some of the region's major foundations to invest with them in the $142 million streetcar project. They raised eyebrows by obtaining public matching funds for a privately sponsored enterprise while the city was cutting services throughout much of the city. Although the "Q" stands for Quicken, the streetcars will move slower than a bus. M-1 was originally designed as a public project to run the length of Woodward Avenue—Detroit's main thoroughfare—from Downtown to the northern city limit and possibly into the suburbs. The privatized QLine will instead run three miles through only the central city areas that are the focus of gentrification. Practicality has given way to the goal of "place-making": the promotion of the boutique project is designed to appeal to tourists and young professionals.[19]

The public transportation needs of Detroit residents, however, extend far out into suburban areas—places where many jobs have relocated but are friendly to neither buses nor pedestrians. In 2015, the *Detroit Free Press* documented the harrowing commute of James Robertson, a 56-year-old black worker from Detroit. Because buses only cover a portion of his transit route to and from his workplace in suburban Rochester Hills, Robertson walks 21 miles daily, often through scorching heat and blistering cold, to his $10.55-an-hour job as an injection molder. Suburbanites, however, have regularly dissociated themselves from the concerns of Detroiters like Robertson, even to the point of having their cities withdraw from the regional SMART bus system in hopes of restricting travel from Detroit. In 2000, only 0.5 percent of the suburbanites in Macomb and Oakland counties said they used public transportation to get to work; only 1 percent reported walking to work. For three decades, Detroit's People Mover, a monorail that only circles Downtown, has been a symbol of the region's failure to cooperate on mass transit in an age when new rail systems were being built elsewhere, such as the San Francisco Bay Area's BART and the METRO in Washington, D.C. It is beyond ironic to see the mocking of the monorail succeeded by hype for the new trolley, which is similarly impractical. The obvious difference is that the much-maligned People Mover is linked to Coleman Young's legacy rather than the city's billionaire saviors.[20]

"Detroit 2.0" is now a full-fledged countertrend to decades of sprawl. Urban density and walking activity have risen alongside new bars, restaurants, and retail outlets. For historian Thomas Sugrue, this amounts only to "trickle-down urbanism," creating a landscape catering to well-off consumers and private enterprise. Gilbert's critics have raised particular concerns over how "safety" considerations are advancing the privatization of space. Most notably, Gilbert has his own private security patrol, with a command center controlling more than 500 cameras monitoring the spaces in and around his buildings. His security team has even installed cameras on buildings Gilbert does not own, without bothering to ask permission. According to the Detroit Police Department, Gilbert's operation is merely the largest of 30 corporate security patrols downtown, 10 of which have command centers. More cops and private security are exactly what is needed, according to conservative *Detroit News* columnist Nolan Finley, who warned that the restrictions on Belle Isle were shifting a "flood of teens" and "rowdies" to Downtown. Their presence "triggered alarm" among the propertied classes whose Downtown investments were premised on "providing a high level of comfort and security to visitors."[21]

Gilbert has also elevated his political investments to correspond with his widened business presence. One of Mayor Mike Duggan's strongest backers, Gilbert joined with his associates at Quicken Loans to donate more than $185,000 to Duggan's campaign, though they were forced to withdraw $80,000 for violating campaign finance law. At the national level, Gilbert has a team of lobbyists in Washington as he continues to vigorously contest federal charges of fraud on subprime mortgages guaranteed by the Federal Housing Administration. Although Quicken Loans did not match the lax standards of the worst predatory lenders, Gilbert's company, according to a 2015 *Detroit News* report, had "the fifth-highest number of mortgages that ended in foreclosure in Detroit over the last decade—and half of those properties are now blighted." A recalcitrant Gilbert, however, derides federal regulators as "govsters." "They just try to extort money from business," he opined. "We will not pay govsters." Although he did not state whom he supported for president in 2016, Gilbert backed Chris Christie in the Republican primary with $1.25 million in campaign contributions because he said he viewed him as "Trump lite."[22]

Undoubtedly the biggest criticism of Gilbert's drive to clean up Downtown has been the charge that his true goal is ethnic cleansing and cultural whitewashing. Amazingly in a city where more than one-third of the landmass is covered by vacant lots and abandoned buildings—as the saying goes, "you could fit San Francisco inside Detroit's empty spaces"—there has been a concerted effort to evict low- to moderate-income residents from structures and locations coveted by private developers.

Capitol Park, a major redevelopment project of Gilbert and his allies, has attracted federal, state, and local government subsidies and financing. When the 127-unit apartment complex at 1214 Griswold was rebranded "The Albert" (after famed architect Albert Kahn), seniors and disabled persons living on fixed incomes were ordered out by March 2014. As of fall 2016, rents ranged from $1,300 a month for a small one-bedroom to $2,565 for a two-bedroom apartment—still cheaper than many other cities but 10 to 20 times what some of the former tenants had paid. Developer Todd Sachse claims he helped pay moving expenses and did the tenants he evicted a favor. "I would bet you that of the 100 people who moved out of here, 95 of them are happier today," Sachse commented. "You can't even wrap your imagination around what this place once looked like—it was beyond a dump."[23]

Evictee Recardo Berrien disagreed. "There's all this hubbub about a 'new Detroit,'" he told journalist Bill McGraw. "I was born and raised in Detroit. For us not to be part of this 'new Detroit' is absurd. We don't see 'us' in none of this. No elderly and poor. We are nowhere in the plans of anyone down here."[24]

A TALE OF TWO CITIES

In November 2005, the Brookings Institution released a report classifying the downtowns of the nation's largest cities according to five typologies. At the top were the "fully developed" downtowns of Manhattan, Chicago, Philadelphia, and Boston. They were followed by cities with downtowns categorized as "emerging," "on the edge of takeoff," and "slow-growing." These middle categories included cities like Pittsburgh and Cleveland, which have regularly been posed as relatively successful examples of Rust Belt redevelopment. Detroit sat at the bottom alongside "declining" downtowns in Cincinnati, Jackson, and St. Louis. This was the "opportunity" that Dan Gilbert and others sensed. "Detroit 2.0" had nowhere to go but up. Today Detroit might qualify as "slow-growing" or perhaps even "on the edge of takeoff."[25]

It is often the case that a declining downtown is symptomatic of citywide disinvestment and economic hardship. The converse, however, does not apply. What the typologies demonstrate is that downtown reinvestment and redevelopment do not in any way ensure better fortunes for working-class people and communities outside of downtown. Even with full development of Chicago's The Loop and Philadelphia's Center City, these cities have continued to face severe crises in public schools, policing, and other forms of social inequality and exclusion. Indeed, downtown development often sucks resources and attention away from the outer neighborhoods.

One of the key questions with which the city has grappled, with increasing fervor, is the value and fairness of subsidizing upper-income residents to relocate to and live in Detroit, when much of the city's population is struggling to survive and stay in their homes. In recent years, Wayne County has set a dubious national record for tax foreclosures, sending 28,000 properties to auction in 2015 and a projected 14,300 more in 2016. The vast majority of these have occurred in Detroit, where residents were hit with a double whammy during the Great Recession and the bank foreclosure crisis. First, they saw their wealth evaporate as their homes plummeted in value. Second, the city government was in such turmoil that it didn't reassess the taxable value of many homes, effectively raising—and in some cases skyrocketing—the property tax rate on the most economically marginalized households. Hundreds of Detroiters found themselves with overdue tax bills that exceeded the value of their homes. Unless a special exemption was granted, they were regularly charged a loan shark's rate of 18 percent interest on back taxes.[26]

In 2010, President Obama launched the Hardest Hit Fund "to help responsible homeowners stay in their homes." Michigan has been one of the top state recipients of the $7.6 billion program. As a result, homeowners who meet certain qualifications could apply for up to $30,000 in interest-free loans and help with mortgage payments, property taxes, and homeowners' association fees. Because of the priorities of Snyder, Orr, and Duggan, however, Michigan gained permission from the federal government to devote most of its Hardest Hit funding to "blight removal." As a result, Detroit has devoted more than $250 million to demolitions, reviving memories of the postwar "slum removal" campaigns that civil rights activists called "Negro removal." Fearing the expansion of "Midtown" gentrification to her North End neighborhood, Michelle Van-Tardy told the *New York Times* in December 2014, "I think it's to make the city look better, not for the citizens, but for the people that they're expecting to come in."[27]

Beyond the debate over the use of Hardest Hit funds, public funding has been devoted to attracting and retaining relatively well-off homeowners through a variety of methods. In particular, subsidies provided to homeowners under the state's Neighborhood Empowerment Zone (NEZ) tax-abatement measures have heavily benefited those in luxury lofts and condominiums, slashing property taxes in the Downtown-Midtown core by more than 90 percent in some cases. For example, owners of a condo in the Book Cadillac (see chapter 4), offered for sale at $465,500 in 2016, were paying annual taxes of only $382. By their own logic, the NEZ tax abatements were intended to be temporary measures to jump-start development and help rehabilitate distressed and blighted structures. However, as developers and well-off homeowners exert their political influence, many are insisting that they be extended in perpetuity. In the meantime, major corporations are devoting their own resources to maintain the momentum for gentrification within the central core. In July 2011, a group of six private employers led by Dan Gilbert's Quicken Loans launched a new program to subsidize their employees' rental or purchase of homes in the Downtown-Midtown area. New buyers were eligible to receive up to $20,000 in forgivable loans, while renters could get $3,500 in cash.[28]

Best characterized by the writing of reporter John Gallagher, the new redevelopment strategy guiding Detroit was designed to concentrate impact, thereby overturning the city council's belief

"that limited resources should go toward those in greatest need."
Wayne State University professor George Galster more bluntly
stated that in order to get "leverage on their investments," local
officials needed to be willing "to pay a little political price to pick
some winners." Detroit wasted its federal funding, he argued, by
giving everyone "a little piece of the pie." Former council member Sheila Cockrel, a one-time Marxist who warmed up to billionaire developers, said this attitude reflected the "social-worker
backgrounds" of council leaders like Erma Henderson and Mar-
yann Mahaffey, pioneering women in Detroit politics. Rooted in
a gendered discourse, the critique of the so-called social-worker
mentality reeks more than a little bit of sexism in its dismissive
attitude toward women politicians lambasted as too soft and too
caring. It privileges the masculinized mastery of abstract data
and statistics, which can be manipulated on paper, in contrast to
the difficult and patient work of communicating, understanding,
and organizing inherent in social work.[29]

In recent years, the city has become increasingly moved by
funding from foundations and private investors insisting on
a "data-driven" and "impact-based" rather than "need-based"
approach to urban investment. In the Downtown-Midtown core,
the ramifications have been inescapable. The obvious problem
with picking "winners," however, is that it also entails picking
"losers." Nearly every resident in Detroit appreciates that the
city has had to figure out ways to make do with shrinking
resources. However, the simultaneous concentration of resources
in a small minority of areas has meant a devastating withdrawal
of resources from neighborhoods deemed "losers." Schools have
been shuttered, streetlights have been turned off, and bus service has been limited. Not surprisingly, housing values have
plummeted—down to almost nothing in the worst-affected

neighborhoods—leading to increased foreclosures, abandonment, and a continuing downward spiral.

Detroit remains a city, however, where such an impact cannot occur without a fight. Formed in 2012, Detroit Eviction Defense has been at the forefront of opposition to the bank and tax foreclosures, advocating "alternative legal strategies and non-profit finance to resist foreclosure." When pro bono services and mediation have proved insufficient to keep Detroiters in their homes, the organization has brought together residents, neighbors, and community supporters in nonviolent direct action against forced evictions. The real-life consequences have been invaluable for families who retained their homes. To be clear, these positive outcomes would need to be multiplied exponentially to change the housing landscape in Detroit. Still, the willingness of homeowners to stand up and speak out against foreclosure proceedings—which are often not just callous but also chaotic and nearly impossible to negotiate—has put a human face on the grim statistics. Together with Detroit Eviction Defense, these homeowners have provided a counter-perspective to the dictates of bankers and financial officials by insisting that the stories and needs of real people and their communities reside at the center of a compassionate response to social crisis.[30]

Many living in the vast sections of the city that have not benefited from the "impact-based" development strategy feel that old injustices are recurring under new names. It is worth recalling that "redlining" was also a data-driven policy directing resources to select neighborhoods while marking others for exclusion. Although explicit racial discrimination is legally prohibited today, private investment and public policy decisions are fostering a disparate impact rooted in implicit bias. Likewise, urban renewal and slum removal once forced thousands of resi-

dents, especially people of color, out of their homes and neighborhoods through condemnation and the invocation of eminent
domain. Now a similar effect is achieved through plans drawn
up by private foundations and sold to public officials desperate
for dollars.

Recalling the Kerner Commission's dire warning a half-century ago, Detroiters Resisting Emergency Management has been
scathing in its critique of the city it sees emerging from warped
priorities inherent in corporate restructuring. The coalition
declared: "The 'revitalized' Detroit is a 'tale of two cities': One
city prosperous and White, the other increasingly poor and African American. Residents of the first are welcomed with open
arms to advance the gentrification of the downtown core."[31]

SIX

From Rebellion to Revolution

Through a long career as a community-based researcher and organizer, Detroit activist Charity Hicks had studied and fought all aspects of injustice: racism, sexism, class exploitation, colonialism, ecological destruction, cultural imperialism, and how multiple forms of oppression intersect. However, in May 2014, Hicks woke to discover that her own Eastside home was the immediate target of the emergency manager's water shutoffs. Homrich Inc. had just received a $5.6 million deal from Kevyn Orr allowing it to claim the funds as fast as it could disconnect customers. People two months behind on bills as small as $150 were placed on the shutoff list.[1]

Without pausing to change clothes or put on shoes, Hicks dashed outside into the brisk morning air. She alerted neighbors to fill up as much water as they could. Insisting there was a mistake, Hicks demanded that the contractor show her the termination order. Instead he sped off, knocking her down and leaving her foot bleeding from a gash. After she called 911 for assistance, the Detroit police carried her off to a state detention center—

bloodied, barefoot, and barely clothed. There she was held for two days in a cell with hundreds of women, one urinal, no seating or bedding, and no drinking or bathing water.[2]

The arrest of Charity Hicks and the accelerating water shutoffs opened up a new chapter in the Detroit bankruptcy. "Initially it was more of a policy struggle," said Tawana Petty, a local organizer and poet. "This made it more of a human struggle where everybody realized just how aggressive it really was." The devastating effects of disenfranchisement and dispossession surfaced in a qualitatively new form, revealing savage water inequities marked by deprivation in Detroit alongside toxic exposure in Flint. Activists reached out to the United Nations, whose investigators declared the water shutoffs a potential violation of international law. National media started paying more attention. "This is a test being looked at by cities across the US—even the world," Hicks declared. "We will not let water be used as a weapon to remake the city in a corporate image. We will re-establish what it is to live in a democracy, with a water system that is part of the commons, that affirms human dignity and that ensures everyone's access."[3]

This final chapter examines Detroit activists, especially African American women activists, working on fundamental matters of human existence from water to food, education, land, sustainable ecology, and community safety. Inspired by Charity's impassioned call to "wage love," they have built movements that push beyond rebellion against an unjust system and toward a revolutionary reconstruction of society from the ground up. Around the globe, tens of millions of people are finding themselves in varying states of precarity and deprived of life's basic necessities as a result of unending war, climate change, and neoliberal dispossession. Building on its long-standing legacy as a movement city, Detroit has become an international model of resilience and creativity in the face of crisis and devastation.

WOMEN'S ACTIVISM AND
A NEW VISION OF LEADERSHIP

One of the most critical forces transforming activism in Detroit since the 1967 rebellion has been the growing presence of leadership by women, especially women of color. Women have undoubtedly fostered greater equity and inclusion within movement organizing. Above and beyond that, as Grace Lee Boggs stated, they have challenged the "patriarchal culture" infecting not only the dominant society but activist circles too:

> Since discovering that the personal is political, women activists have been abandoning the charismatic male, vertical, and vanguard party leadership patterns of the 1960s and creating more participatory, empowering, and horizontal kinds of leadership. Instead of modeling their organizing on the lives of men outside the home—for example, in the plant or in the political arena—they are beginning to model it on the love, caring, healing, and patience that, along with an appreciation of diversity and of strengths and weaknesses, go into the raising of a family.[4]

The struggle over water has been a prime example of the impact of women's activism and leadership. Based in Detroit, the Michigan Welfare Rights Organization (MWRO) first brought public attention to the problem of water shutoffs and privatization during the state takeover of Highland Park, a small municipality geographically located within the heart of Detroit. One of MWRO's founders and veteran leaders is Marian Kramer, who has been a fixture in Detroit's activist community dating back to the Black Power movement. Raised in Louisiana, Kramer became a student activist within the southern civil rights movement. After moving to Detroit, she became a central figure in the Dodge Revolutionary Union Movement and the League of Revolutionary Black Workers—all the while challenging sexism and the unequal, gendered division of labor within organizations that purported to be radical.[5]

Kramer has been joined in the MWRO by African American and Latina organizers like Maureen Taylor and Sylvia Orduño, who have provided leadership to a wide range of movement activity in Detroit and worked with a broad coalition of Detroiters to host nearly 20,000 activists for the 2010 United States Social Forum. In their practice, welfare has been far more than a single-issue focus. Instead, it is a cornerstone from which to engage the postindustrial proletariat, which is now far less likely to be working in the factory and far more likely to be structurally unemployed. Welfare rights organizing also provides a vantage point from which to condemn the workings of a political and economic system that produces unemployment, poverty, and homelessness. Importantly, these struggles empower the voices of women of color who have borne the brunt of the neoliberal assault. Not only have they suffered cuts to material benefits for them and their children, they have also endured the racist, sexist stereotyping of "welfare queens" by those ideologically determined to end the era of "big government."

Formed in 2008, the People's Water Board brought MWRO and 30 other labor, environmental, antiracist, faith-based, and human rights organizations together to protect water in southeast Michigan from the threats of pollution, commodification, and privatization. In the face of tens of thousands of shutoffs, the coalition has called for the Detroit Water and Sewer Department to implement the water affordability plan, which MWRO pushed the city council to adopt in 2005 but which the department has yet to enact. Drawing on the experience of other cities, the plan would scale water charges based on the income of ratepayers rather than a flat fee for all. The heightened resistance has won significant concessions, including an intermittent moratorium and new grants to aid severely impoverished residents. The water shutoffs, however, have remained an ongoing source of controversy and struggle with far-reaching consequences. Unpaid water bills are added to property taxes, rendering houses subject to foreclosure. Homes with disconnected water are deemed "blighted" and placed on the demolition list. Furthermore, water shutoffs create unsanitary conditions that can cause health problems and subject parents and guardians to having their children taken away by Child Protective Services.[6]

The decision whether to continue shutoffs or adopt a feasible plan for water affordability, therefore, serves as a symbol of greater societal values. The struggles over water have brought to light the human dimensions of what is at stake when neoliberal measures are imposed on cities deemed to be in financial distress. Is water, as the UN and leading Detroit activists argue, a sacred resource and a human right that cannot be abridged without risking crimes against humanity? Or is access to water ultimately subject to market forces and political directives?

Grassroots organizing around water and other essentials of human life builds on the legacy of cooperative acts that sustained the black community through the Montgomery Bus Boycott. Collective actions also reprise and update the work of the unemployment councils that brought Detroiters, and Americans, together during the Great Depression. Through humanitarian gestures, those councils projected values that would later become institutionalized through government programs like Social Security, Unemployment Insurance, Aid to Families with Dependent Children, and Medicare. In the age of neoliberal dispossession, residents today have improvised what *Bloomberg* reporter Valerie Vande Panne termed a "neighborly safety net" in which "the city's neglected poor rely on time banking, skill-sharing, and giveaways to get by."[7]

Contemporary Detroit activists recognize that they must address urgent human needs while setting examples of a more humane, democratic, sustainable, and mutualistic way of living. Through MWRO, the People's Water Board, and a diverse body of organizations—including We the People of Detroit, Detroit People's Platform, Boggs Center to Nurture Community Leadership, Allied Media Projects, and Detroiters Resisting Emergency Management—women and gender-nonconforming activists of color demonstrate that people on the margins can and must exercise the power to shape their own destiny. They have developed concrete plans and missions informed by research, theoretical discussions, and on-the-ground listening and organizing.

While unafraid to confront authority, visionary organizers have moved from the "rejections" defining the stage of rebellion to the "projections" necessary to revolutionize the way we live, work, and sustain community. Nonviolent direct action and civil disobedience have disrupted callous attempts to deprive residents of water and housing, while exposing the values and operations of the neoliberal order. At the same time, acts of direct aid by residents and neighbors—sharing water, food, and lodging between households, donating thousands of gallons of water and other bases of subsistence, and growing food on vacant lots—have created new models and networks of interpersonal and social solidarity.

Putting things in historical and philosophical perspective, Grace Lee Boggs declared, "Today's cultural revolution, which is emerging from the ground up especially in Detroit, is as awesome as the transitions from hunting and gathering to agriculture eleven thousand years ago and from agriculture to industry a few hundred years ago." Boggs saw the wreckage of the counter-revolution as a sign of the old industrial order dying. However, in her late nineties, she began to see a new promise in the technology that had eliminated factory jobs in the Rust Belt. Visitors to her home were given copies of a *Smithsonian* article citing technologists who believe that "3-D printing will democratize design and free us from the hegemony of mass manufacturing." Hundreds attended conferences in Detroit sponsored by the Boggs Center to "reimagine work" by returning to permacultural practices and leaping forward into the age of digital fabrication.[8]

This combination of urban food cultivation and machines that can be programmed to make most of life's material necessities can offer the proletariat a new method to own the means of production. Black entrepreneurs in Detroit, like Blair Evans, insist that the technology and human capacity already exist to liberate workers from corporate employment and foster self-reliance for historically marginalized communities. What Detroit's most creative organizers thus stress is building the social consciousness and relationships necessary to unleash the greatest potential of the postindustrial epoch.[9]

EDUCATION TO GOVERN

The contrast between the depth of compassion and conviction evident within social movements and the top-down thinking that promises quick fixes has been particularly apparent in the realm of education, where a slew of problematic emergency managers have taken turns for more than a decade. With the future of education in Detroit rendered uncertain by the chaotic imposition of "school choice," the activist response to the crisis of Detroit Public Schools (DPS) has produced resistance and alternatives.

The direct opposition to charter schools and emergency management has been led by the elected members of the DPS school board "in exile," who have consistently fought to regain "community control" in the name of black and brown Detroiters. They have waged legal and political challenges to the state takeover, rampant school closures, and mismanagement of funds. Moreover, they have been sharply critical of local and minority entrepreneurs and professionals they see as colluding with the hostile takeover.[10]

In September 2016, a group of parents working with public-interest lawyers from Public Counsel filed a federal class-action suit against Snyder and state officials. "The lawsuit documents pervasive, shock-the-conscience conditions that deny children the opportunity to attain literacy, including lack of books, classrooms without teachers, insufficient desks, buildings plagued by vermin, unsafe facilities and extreme temperatures," said attorney Kathryn Eidmann. "One seventh- and eighth-grade classroom was taught for a month by an eighth-grade student." While there are mountains of evidence that students are suffering, legal efforts thus far have failed to overturn the emergency manager law or hold the state liable for major damages to DPS. Indeed, the state's official position is that children have no right to literacy and no basis to seek a court remedy.[11]

While generally sympathetic to the quest to restore "community control," a third group of activists has emphasized the imperative to transform curriculum and pedagogy, which, they insist, is necessary even with autonomy and resources. After the closure of the cause célèbre school, Catherine Ferguson Academy, the James and Grace Lee Boggs School emerged as a beacon of hope and possibility to parents, educators, and organizers inspired by the Boggses' vision of "education to govern." Grace Lee Boggs gave her blessing for the school to a much younger generation of founders, many of whom were teachers frustrated by the limitations of the current system. Three women from diverse backgrounds, Julia Putnam, Amanda Rosman, and Marisol Teachworth, opened the school in 2013 after meeting and planning for many years through a group set up to promote "freedom schooling."

Born and raised in the city, Julia Putnam (who would become principal of Boggs School) was the first volunteer to sign up for Detroit Summer in 1992, leading her into the revolutionary world of James and Grace Lee Boggs. Deindustrialization, the Boggses argued, had made working-class youth, especially urban black youth, expendable to the capitalist system. Jobs disappeared as corporations outsourced production in search of inexpensive labor. Higher education, offered up as the solution, was only increasing alienation and stratification. For instance, as the University of Michigan prioritized its pursuit of wealthy white students paying out-of-state tuition, it became nearly off-limits for black and brown Detroiters. Its enrollment of black students from Wayne County diminished to a trickle—just 86 students (1 percent) out of a class of 6,071 freshmen in fall 2015. The Boggses believed that urban youth, so often feared and scorned, could be the center of a movement "to rebuild, revitalize, and respirit Detroit from the ground up."[12]

"There are very few things," Putnam remembered, "I have been so sure of as knowing that I would be a part of Detroit

Summer." It was an eye-opening and life-changing decision for a teenager. "How are we going to fix the world's problems?" Grace Lee Boggs asked her, while Jimmy Boggs told Putnam and her peers that "if we were going to make a difference, it would have to be about more than money."[13]

Putnam joined with other youth participants to transform vacant lots into gardens and paint murals of social justice over landscapes of abandonment. They hosted community dinners with local organizers and continued deep into the evening with intergenerational dialogs about the city's past, present, and future. Detroit Summer focused on the role of youth as change agents— people who worked with veteran activists and community elders to think creatively, apply skills, and develop self-capacity to tackle and solve social problems. Inspired by Mississippi Freedom Summer and the ideas of radical educators like Paulo Freire, the principles of the summer "freedom schooling" project were manifested two decades later through the Boggs School.

Whereas others promise (often falsely) to help urban youth move up within the world of education and the global capitalist order, the Boggses maintained that our existing academic and economic systems were set up to promote exploitation and dehumanization. It was neither feasible nor desirable to make them equitable; Detroit needed to become the model for a paradigm shift in education. Along those lines, the Boggs School established place-based learning that emphasizes building and valuing community and social justice. "The problem now is that so many young people think that success means being able to get out of Detroit," declared Putnam. "Part of what we want to do is redefine what it means to be successful."[14]

The early years of the Boggs School have revealed the stress and magic of visionary organizing in Detroit. To open on time, the school rushed to find a location, eventually securing an old settlement-house building that required extensive rehabbing. It is located in the shadow of the nation's largest municipal incinerator, which has proved to be both an environmental and a financial disaster for the city. Not surprisingly, the school's surrounding neighborhood has been heavily depopulated.

All these forces arrayed against the school, however, make its efforts that much more meaningful. The Boggs School has become a symbol of the new city that is possible when Detroit's people are seen as assets rather than liabilities and when exclusion from the existing order is taken as an opening to explore Martin Luther King Jr.'s radical revolution of values. One of its already legendary stories gives a sense of how it is uniquely treasured. One day, school officials found a student visibly sick and decided he needed to be sent home. When they called his mother, she was shocked to discover he was not in his bed. The sick boy had snuck out of the house because he loved school too much to stay home.[15]

Perhaps the worst disservice one can do to a local success story is to take it out of context and blow it out of proportion. Even the greatest schools in Detroit—including those with the type of phenomenal family and community support network the Boggs School has marshaled—face ongoing challenges. In a sign of stark reality, the Boggs School's founders made the difficult and controversial decision to apply for a charter. With the emergency manager contracting DPS, and private school costs being prohibitive for most Detroit families, they concluded it was the only means possible. Ironically, it was the right wing's chaotic rush toward charters that opened a crack in the door for a school based on the ideas of revolutionary activists. This irony has not been lost on conservatives, who have cited the Boggs School's success as a rationale for gutting public schools even further. Rejecting the privatization agenda of leading charter advocates, the school's founders have tried to build public and community accountability into its mission. The Boggs School is managed as a nonprofit organization and does none of the conspicuous poaching from DPS or garish marketing that other charters engage in. One of the only pro-union charter schools in Michigan, its employees play a cooperative role in planning and governance.[16]

Nevertheless, the greater future of education in Detroit depends on small pilot schools being more than boutique successes or alternatives. Detroiters continue to struggle to build a movement that can apply the best lessons obtainable to revive a public school system that is rooted in the realities and concerns of a majority black and working-class city. To have a truly transformative impact, schools like this must ultimately be connected to equally visionary movements for housing, health care, child care, food justice, community safety, public transportation, spiritual well-being, and cooperative economics. This is the true opportunity within crisis that Detroit now represents.

FREEING THE LAND

Recalling the unmet demand for freedmen to receive 40 acres and a mule during Reconstruction, the struggle for land has deep historical, political, and cultural roots within the collective consciousness of African Americans. In the years of the Black Power movement, the drive to reclaim the historic homeland in the South animated the organizing of the Republic of New Africa, whose legacy can be seen in the movement to make Jackson, Mississippi, a base of black self-determination and solidarity economics. On a related front, the Boggses stressed the idea that "the city is the black man's land" to outline a strategy for black control of urban politics.

Building on these legacies, the movement to free the land in Detroit has grown to address concerns about environmental justice, sustainable community, food sovereignty, and cooperative economics. It is a movement most publicized and best exemplified by urban farming, which has developed into a wider and deeper phenomenon than typically suggested by the idea of community gardens. Urban farming in Detroit drew initial inspiration from African American elders, many raised in the rural South, who worked through organizations like the Gardening Angels and the urban 4-H Club and connected with youth in Detroit Summer and school-based farming programs. Since the 1990s, hundreds of farms and gardens have sprouted up in the city. Many were started by neighbors working on small plots of land, but a growing number have been planted by residents and migrants who have moved to Detroit specifically to be part of the farming community.[17]

The city's veteran gardeners saw the vast expanse of vacant lots and abandonment as an opening and opportunity, but the issue of what to do with those presumed vacant spaces has become increasingly contentious over the past decade. On one hand, the Heidelberg Project has demonstrated the communal value of abandoned spaces. Artist Tyree Guyton transformed vacant lots and dilapidated homes on the Eastside streets where he grew up into an internationally renowned public art space through the creation of found-object installations—what some would call repurposed trash. On the other hand, the Marathon Oil refinery saw the combination of vacant space and economic hardship as an opportunity to expand its toxic operations in Southwest Detroit. In 2007, after threatening to direct new investment to its Minnesota or Illinois sites, Marathon secured a $175 million tax abatement, which the city approved in the elusive quest to restore industrial employment. The company invested $2.2 billion to bolster its processing by an extra 17,000 barrels of oil per day. However, an investigation by the *Detroit Free Press* found that Marathon's employment of Detroit residents only grew from 15 workers in 2007 to 30 in 2014—at a cost of nearly $12 million per job.[18]

Although its economic impact is questionable, Marathon's expansion has had devastating effects on both local residential neighborhoods and the global struggle against climate change. Southwest Detroit, the historic center of the city's Mexican American and Latinx community, has been continuously hampered by industrial encroachment, including freeway construction and the heightened volume of commercial trucks crossing the U.S.-Canadian bridge. The Delray neighborhood, known as Little Hungary before World War II, has lost over 90 percent of its population. While Marathon bought out some relieved homeowners, it has made no offers or concessions to residents in the predominantly black Boynton neighborhood located just across the freeway from the refinery and in the center of the state's most polluted zip code. Their homes rendered all but worthless, Boynton residents report dizziness, difficulty breathing, and feeling overwhelmed by noxious smells even when they are indoors with their windows sealed. Tests have shown elevated levels of lung and bronchus cancer.[19]

The intensified pollution is a product of Marathon's expansion to refine the significantly dirtier Canadian tar sands—the same product the Keystone XL pipeline was designed to transport to the Gulf of Mexico. Indigenous activists and environmentalists moved to block Keystone XL, defining it as an

existential threat to First Nations and the biosphere. Nevertheless, the tar sands not only have flowed to Detroit, they also
caused the disastrous July 2010 spill in the Kalamazoo River—
the worst inland oil spill in U.S. history. The toxic dumping on
Detroiters reached a new level of outrageousness and absurdity
when a massive pile of petroleum coke, a byproduct of tar sands
refining, emerged on the banks of the Detroit River in 2013. The
coke was actually owned by Koch Industries, which was storing
it for shipment to countries in the Global South as one of the
dirtiest, high-carbon-emitting sources of energy on the planet.[20]

The implication that Detroit is so desperate for jobs that corporations can get away with just about anything has even infested
the urban farming movement. Wealthy finance capitalist John
Hantz has championed himself as the pioneer of large-scale, for-
profit urban agriculture in Detroit, promising to restore economic vitality and rid the city of blight. In December 2012, the
city council narrowly approved, over adamant protest, an initial
contract to sell Hantz nearly 2,000 city-owned parcels of land
spanning 200 acres on the Eastside. In what critics deemed a
landgrab and sweetheart deal, Hantz purchased the acreage
without appraisal for only eight cents per square foot. He has
stated an objective to own 10,000 acres in Detroit and a belief that
the city needs several equally large corporate-owned farms.
When Kevyn Orr took office, he expressed the utmost support
and confidence in Hantz. Mike Score, president of Hantz Farms,
insists the company has been "slandered" by activists with an
"ideological" ax to grind.[21]

Urban agriculture is ultimately a means to an end for Hantz,
who has explicitly acknowledged his desire to reshape the real
estate market by maneuvering to "create scarcity," drive up
property values, and increase private land ownership. Farming,

Hantz assessed, is a "cheap" way to achieve these intentions. He further insisted that a for-profit farm is essential to demonstrating the future economic viability of the city. Yet, in another only-in-Detroit act carried out with no hint of irony, Hantz launched his grand plan to bring back "jobs" and inspire "entrepreneurialism" by calling for 1,200 volunteers to plant 15,000 baby trees on his privately owned land. In what has become an annual event, Hantz primarily draws whites from the suburbs to support his endeavors. It is a truly audacious move, analogous to a private corporation purchasing Habitat for Humanity to run it as a money-making venture, yet still asking hundreds of volunteers to provide free labor as a charitable act. The symbolism of volunteers aiding a wealthy white man in a city that is deeply impoverished and predominantly black is jarring.[22]

Most of the activists at the core of Detroit's urban farming movement have viewed the initiatives of Hantz and similarly minded businessmen as a bastardization of their work. Lottie Spady, then of the East Michigan Environmental Action Council, argued that "the concept of large-scale commercial farming" was antithetical to the principles of environmental justice, particularly given that it had "not been vetted or test-driven in an urban area." Malik Yakini of the Detroit Black Community Food Security Network challenged Hantz's aim of making land scarce for private gain. As an organizer of the D-Town Farm, covering seven acres of leased public land on the Westside, he emphasized the importance of urban farming to promote community empowerment and self-determination. Yakini and others in the Detroit Food Policy Council pursued the goal of food sovereignty in which Detroiters and all people reclaim the human right to produce and consume healthy, sustainable, slow food in the face of the industrialization and monopolization of food by the likes of Monsanto, Walmart, and McDonald's. Consistent with that goal, Charity Hicks called for the land to be placed into community land trusts, a nonprofit structure by which members of the community could control and determine the use of land in perpetuity, based on peoples' needs rather than market value.[23]

Countering the image of the city as a "blank slate" in need of "Great Man" saviors like Gilbert and Hantz, urban farming for many Detroiters embodies the "quiet strength" of the city's most storied transplant, Rosa Parks. It is not flashy or self-promoting but deeply rooted and life-sustaining—creating profound connections among the people. Setting down roots in the Jefferson-Chalmers neighborhood on the city's eastern edge just beyond Hantz's operations, the Feedom Freedom Growers have demonstrated the radical potential of grassroots urban farming. (Their name was inspired by the black farmers' motto that we can't free ourselves unless we can feed ourselves.) In a part of town that was once anchored by three major auto factories but has been reduced to one heavily downsized Chrysler plant, vacant lots now predominate on many blocks where the neighborhood's 7,500 housing units stood in 1960.[24]

Founded by lifelong Detroiters Myrtle Thompson-Curtis and former Black Panther Wayne Curtis, Feedom Freedom has transformed one acre of vacant lots into a center of hope and community. Answering the call to create "a whole new culture" out of postindustrial despair, the farm serves to remediate the soil, beautify the blighted landscape, and provide fresh food in a part of town where gas stations and liquor stores vastly outnumber quality grocery stores. More than that, Feedom Freedom is an educational project—teaching not only healthy eating but also food justice and black culture. The farm is an anchor of community life and successfully joined with Detroit Eviction Defense to stop the dispossession of the home of a neighbor facing foreclosure.

These small-scale farms exemplify Detroit activists' concept of movement building-blocks that are an "inch wide and a mile deep." They repudiate John Hantz's notion that places without market value are devoid of potential. While local policy makers have not swallowed this mentality whole, they have embraced its neoliberal essence. As geographer Sara Safransky noted in 2014, city planners and private foundations working from a "data-driven" approach have relied on a superficial "market value analysis" of real estate to determine which Detroit neighborhoods should be bolstered or depleted. The result was a thick and glossy compendium of urban design called *Detroit Future City,* which the emergency manager adopted as the imperative for "right-sizing" the city in conjunction with corporate restructuring.[25]

Public investment is now targeted and private investment incentivized in "steady" and "low vacancy" areas. The Detroit Land Bank further serves to put publicly owned properties back into private hands within such areas. By contrast, Thompson-Curtis learned that Feedom Freedom's location on Manistique Street had been categorized by the city as an "urban homestead" territory. The designation was a key example of how city planning has been inspired by visionary green concepts but has put them in service of neoliberal dispossession. "Urban homestead" areas are often "distressed" sites where services are projected to be cut (e.g., school closures, reduced street lighting, limited public transportation). Many of these "high vacancy" neighborhoods, where 90,000 people still live, are to be rezoned for green purposes, such as forests to act as a carbon sink or retention ponds to capture storm water.[26]

For farms like Feedom Freedom, however, it is the prevalence of land with limited or no market value that creates an opening for alternative values to take hold. By making productive use of land that would otherwise be gobbled up on the cheap by speculators, the farm demonstrates the use value of vacated space to serve the community and form the basis for noncommercial economic relations.

BLACK LIVES STILL MATTER

We close with the issue that touched off the powder keg in 1967. Despite major steps to integrate the police department and elevate African Americans into leadership positions, police brutality has remained a persistent and deadly problem in Detroit. From 1987 to 2000, the city paid out $124 million in response to lawsuits over police misconduct. Police were killing Detroit residents at the highest rate of any major American city: 47 people died between 1995 and 2000. These included notorious cases of victims killed by "boomerang bullets": the police claimed to fire in self-defense at people they shot in the back. The killings continued as the department routinely conducted shoddy investigations that relied on the word of police officers while dismissing conflicting evidence and witness accounts. Officer Eugene Brown was the human embodiment of excessive force. He was involved in nine shooting incidents within six years and killed three people under suspicious circumstances on three separate occasions in less than two years. Citizens also complained of being put in choke holds, punched in the ribs, slammed headfirst into a car, and kneed in the groin. In every case, Brown was cleared of wrongdoing. Staunchly defended by the police union, he even sued and received a court-ordered promotion to sergeant in 2004.[27]

Since 1996, the Detroit Coalition Against Police Brutality (DCAPB) has served as the community voice of conscience on policing matters, working with victims of police abuse and their families while pressing for effective citizen oversight of police. Formed in response to the infamous police killing of Malice Green, the coalition was founded by veteran activists Ron Scott, Gloria House, and Marge Parsons, whose collective history traced back to formative 1960s organizations like the Black Panther Party and the Student Nonviolent Coordinating Committee. Through a combination of advocacy by DCAPB and exposés by investigative journalists, Mayor Dennis Archer requested a federal investigation of the Detroit Police Department in 2000 that resulted in a 2003 consent decree. The department committed to carry out major reforms and was kept under federal oversight until 2016.[28]

Giving testimony on how Eugene Brown stole the life of her son, Arnetta Grable emerged as a key public spokesperson lending moral force to DCAPB. Gunned down in 1996, Lamar Grable, a young African American man who volunteered with the NAACP and aspired to be a writer, never reached his 21st birthday. Autopsy results contradicted Brown's claim that Grable was fighting him face-to-face when he shot him, and there was no evidence of Grable's fingerprints on the gun Brown claimed he possessed. Lamar was shot seven times, including twice in the back and three more times in the chest at point-blank range with his back likely pressed against the ground. Carrying her son's story to Washington, Arnetta Grable camped in the hallway of the Department of Justice and refused to leave until she met with Attorney General Janet Reno. After securing the federal investigation, she moved forward with a civil lawsuit and turned down a $2.25 million settlement to ensure her day in court. This prompted her own lawyers to file a motion asking the court to declare her incompetent and make them guardians of her son's estate. Undeterred, Grable found new lawyers and won a jury verdict that held up on appeal all the way to the state supreme court. The resulting judgment against the city ultimately amounted to $6 million.[29]

Grable's tireless activism exemplifies the central and indispensible role black women have played in the struggle against both violence within the community and state-sanctioned violence. During the 1980s, African American mothers of murdered children drew a new level of awareness and depth of concern for the problem of youth violence through the formation of SOSAD: Save our Sons and Daughters. This grassroots vision of nurturing community carried over into the organizing against police brutality, where the concerns of black mothers and guardians remained central. In the 2015 activist guide *How to End Police Brutality,* Ron Scott provided a clear sense of DCAPB's approach, writing that "courage and mediation [are equally as] important as confrontation and retaliation in resolving dangerous situations." As a cofounder of the Detroit chapter of the Black Panthers, Scott had embraced the party's militant line against the police occupation of black communities but had prioritized survival programs as key to building the people's capacity for self-organization and self-government. This same philosophy and strategy has informed DCAPB's signature program of building and renewing "Peace Zones 4 Life."[30]

Here again, a gendered analysis of organizing in response to these "dangerous situations" was crucial. Community violence regularly resulted from disputes between men, some of which started as responses to minor indiscretions or indignities that escalated into deadly confrontations. At the same time, DCAPB found that acts of police violence and killing regularly occurred after residents called the police to help resolve domestic conflicts. Thus, the intent of Peace Zones 4 Life is to develop deescalation and conflict-resolution skills within the community, while imparting a collective sense of purpose through neighborhood projects and cooperative economic activity. While we have witnessed a rash and unending stream of police killings nationwide, unarmed DCAPB members have successfully intervened to resolve potentially deadly encounters—raising expectations of what the community should expect and demand from its professionally trained law enforcement.

On the surface, this approach may be seen as a call for devoting greater attention to what the mainstream media and politicians call "black-on-black violence." The point, however, is not to develop a "blame the victim" mentality or absolve the state of its culpability for creating the conditions under which such violence occurs. Instead, the goal is to spread the revolutionary idea—consistent with calls for transformative justice and the abolition of police—that self-determining communities can create healthy models of human relationships that make calling the police increasingly unnecessary. This goal overlaps with that of activist women of color who have struggled to decriminalize domestic violence and intimate partner violence, moving beyond retributive state actions that strive to punish offenders but that ultimately harm their families and communities as well.[31]

While the federally mandated reforms and emergent Peace Zones have significantly slowed the pace of police killings in Detroit, they have not ended them. Post-9/11 moves toward militarization have raised a new sense of alarm, as has the continued problem of police and vigilante murders in the suburbs. In line with the women/queer leadership and emphasis on holistic and intersectional analysis of the national Movement for Black Lives, Detroit activists have highlighted the targeting of black women and girls while pointing to the significance of gender, sexuality, and class. In one of the most notorious police shootings in recent memory nationwide, seven-year-old Aiyana Stanley-Jones was sleeping on the sofa on May 16, 2010, when the Detroit SWAT team errantly stormed her Eastside home in a midnight raid while looking for a suspect who lived in a different apartment unit. Officer Joseph Weekley—mistakenly, he claimed—shot her in the head with his submachine gun. What made her death even more egregious was the strong suspicion that the SWAT team took extra-dramatic and rash actions, such as firing a flashbang grenade, because it was being filmed for *The First 48,* a reality television show on the A&E channel. After two trials had ended with a hung jury, the judge dismissed the felony manslaughter charged and the prosecutor asked to drop the final misdemeanor charge against Weekley, who returned to active duty in 2015.[32]

Two more outrageous murders occurred in suburbs of Detroit. In October 2011, Shelly Hilliard, a 19-year-old black transgender woman from Detroit, was brutally killed after officers from the Madison Heights Police Department and the Oakland County Narcotics Enforcement Team used her as an informant and discarded her. Known to her friends as Treasure, she was nabbed by cops who saw her smoking a joint on the balcony of a Motel 6, where she engaged in sex work. Facing charges of possession of half an ounce of marijuana, Hilliard was coerced to set up her dealer, under fear she would be sent to a male prison. She cooperated with the police to secure the dealer's arrest; however, in a wantonly irresponsible act, the authorities leaked her name to the dealer, who had been arrested with an associate. Soon released from jail, they exacted revenge by torturing and dismembering Hilliard, then dumped her torso near the side of a freeway and set it on fire. Although the killers were imprisoned, the cops who set her up faced no charges. The horrendous chain of events prompted a heightened level of trans awareness and advocacy, much of which has emanated from the Ruth Ellis Center, a community shelter and agency for queer and trans youth in Detroit.[33]

In November 2013, a new wave of community activism erupted following the killing of Renisha McBride, another 19-year-old black woman from Detroit. After getting into a car accident near the Detroit city border, McBride became disoriented and, in the early morning, knocked on the door of a Dearborn Heights resident asking for help. Theodore Wafer instead shot her in the face through his screen door. As the police were not directly involved, McBride's death recalled the killing of Trayvon Martin. Activists drew public attention to the case to get ahead of any attempt to defend Wafer's shooting as a "stand your ground" act à la George Zimmerman. In this instance, McBride's vigilante killer was convicted of three charges, including second-degree murder, and sentenced to 17 to 32 years in prison.[34]

While community advocates found this outcome more satisfactory than those of prior cases, it was not a reason to celebrate or rest. The living memories of Aiyana, Treasure, Renisha, and so many others remind Detroiters of the ongoing problem of violence that has yet to be resolved. Their names and images have been held aloft in banners for the continued efforts of DCAPB to build Peace Zones 4 Life, the sadly necessary demonstrations to assert that Black Lives Matter, and the jubilant and strategic gatherings of the Allied Media Conference (AMC). One of the Detroit organizing community's signature events, the AMC draws more than 2,000 activists from the city and the nation each summer.

Heartbreakingly, the activists who have elevated the victims of tragedies were beset with a series of devastating losses among their own ranks. In May 2014, Charity Hicks traveled to New York City to raise awareness of Detroit's water struggle at the Left Forum conference. While waiting for a bus in Midtown Manhattan, she was struck and killed by a reckless driver who jumped the curb and fled the scene. Several months later, Grace Lee Boggs fell in her home and entered extended hospice care. When she passed on October 5, 2015, the once marginal radical was immediately recognized by obituaries in every local and national news publication conceivable. Even President Obama weighed in with a public tribute. One month after the community celebrated Boggs's unlikely and phenomenal journey, Ron Scott passed away from natural causes. All of these commanding figures represented the heart and soul of their communities. Their work and spirit live on in the slow and patient organizing to make a more democratic and humane city arise from catastrophe.

Detroit activists like Yusef Bunchy Shakur are carrying forward this legacy of philosophical activism with the conviction that transformational models of love and healing are vital to community building and movement organizing. Shakur came of age during the height of the drug wars as a gang leader and self-identified "thug" in the Zone 8 neighborhood—not far from the center of the 1967 rebellion. It was a place, as he described in his autobiography, populated by "broken human beings" who saw "criminal behavior as their only means of survival in their hellish reality." After bouncing in and out of schools and juvenile detention, Shakur was sent to prison at the age of 19 for a crime he swore he did not commit. There he was mentored by his father for the first time, began devouring every book he could get his hands on, and turned to Malcolm X as a model of "transformation and redemption." Shakur left prison as a "revolutionary" activist determined "to be a difference maker in my community."[35]

A decade-and-a-half later, he is one of the most respected community organizers and organic intellectuals in the city. As the founder and organizer of the annual "Restoring the Neighbor Back to the 'Hood" event, Shakur provides backpacks, school supplies, and community educational programs for thousands of school-aged children and their families. It is a prime example of his efforts to identify and draw out of today's youth the potential that few managed to see in him as a child. Shakur also works with formerly incarcerated persons to help them regain productive and stable lives, while advocating for structural changes to end the school-to-prison pipeline and dismantle the prison industrial complex. He is building relationships that bridge many of the city's greatest divides—race, class, gender, sexuality, and geography—in order to rebuild self-reliant and self-determining communities.

In the end, like so many other diverse grassroots activists outside of the spotlight who have refused to quit on themselves or Detroit, Shakur opens our eyes to the difficult but history-making work that marches forward against all odds: "We have all realized that we have to stand together, organize around one heartbeat and speak with one voice as a unified Detroit through community outreach programs, which are impacting, educating and empowering the people. It is an ongoing struggle for us all to put our ideological and petty differences aside and come together for the betterment of the people of Detroit, because the world is watching us and anticipating our glory."[36]

Conclusion

Since the settlement of Detroit's bankruptcy, the key financial strategist behind it has openly boasted of the precedent-setting nature of his work in talks across the globe. Known as a cutthroat, corporate "turnaround king" on Wall Street, Kenneth Buckfire cites Detroit as a model for the application of corporate restructuring methods within the public sector, specifically dictating neoliberal measures he believes should be applied to Puerto Rico. The primary goal should always be spurring private investment. This requires restoring the confidence of investors by paying "secured" Wall Street creditors in full while gutting pensions, neutralizing unions, and beating down democratic opposition.[1]

Buckfire's global victory tour is a sign of how financial scheming that was once carried out behind closed doors—surfacing only when turncoats published tell-all books with titles like *Confessions of an Economic Hit Man*—is now brazenly packaged within a set of dictates we all must follow.[2] Yet, as extreme as his "shock doctrine" views may seem, American political culture is being pushed even further to the right by climate change denial, white nationalism, xenophobia, and authoritarianism.

Popularized by British prime minister Margaret Thatcher, the mantra of neoliberalism has been "there is no alternative." The collapse of Detroit, a one-time stronghold of labor and civil rights, should awaken us to see how much the promise of freedom under neoliberalism not only carries hidden costs for ourselves but also comes at the cost of coercive behavior toward others. The drive to put a price tag on every aspect of life and subject it all to the winning and losing outcomes of the commercial market has intensified the suffering of those who are poor, elderly, disabled, and most vulnerable in society. It has breathed new life into the "survival of the fittest" discourse that gave rise to Social Darwinism and scientific racism.

The showdown in Detroit, seeking to bring what I have called a 50-year rebellion to a decisive end, is thus a prologue of the showdown for the United States and the world. Schools, communities, cities, states, and nations spanning the globe are confronting the crises wrought by privatization, financialization, and dispossession. While Detroiters are dealing with the aftermath of deindustrialization, the people in Standing Rock, Chiapas, Palestine, and many other sites are struggling against neoliberal dispossession to preserve indigenous lands and cultures. Unfettered trade and commercialization have created an ecological crisis and spurred toxic forms of nationalism in reaction.

From a global perspective, we can see the economic dislocation and chaos that neoliberalism has sown in Detroit building steam as it rolls on. The loss of work in the Rust Belt to outsourcing has resulted in rapid and chaotic industrialization in China, where labor, feminist, human rights, and environmental activists are grappling with a qualitatively new set of problems and consequences. In 2010, the massive Shenzhen complex where iPhones are made was home to 420,000 of Foxconn Technology's 800,000 employees in China—dwarfing the peak industrial-era employment figures of Ford and its River Rouge plant. Symbolizing the traumatic rupture of life in China, Foxconn was moved to install safety nets surrounding its buildings to stop dejected workers from leaping to their deaths. Industrialization has proceeded on such an accelerated timetable in China that workers are already facing the calamitous effects of automation and outsourcing. One factory making cell phone parts in Dongguan downsized its workforce from 650 employees to 60 by using robots to boost productivity by 162 percent. Transnational firms are also shifting labor-intensive work to Vietnam and Bangladesh, where the wage rates are more than 50 and 75 percent cheaper, respectively, than those in China.[3]

The globalization of production and capital flight have challenged Detroit activists to respond to this increasingly transnational character of capitalism. They bring to their work an immense amount of pride in the city and their local communities. Nevertheless, their localism rejects the parochialism of NIMBY ("not-in-my-backyard") activism, which works not to remedy social problems but merely push them onto less privileged communities. It is also not interested in becoming "equal" to suburbs produced by racial segregation and sprawl. Instead, it is an intercommunal form of localism that seeks to connect with place-based struggles around the globe that refuse to be absorbed into a dehumanizing and unsustainable system.

Having traced the ways in which our current crisis began in Detroit, I conclude with clarity rather than certainty. The end of reform is heightening contradictions, removing the reformist middle path, and pushing us back toward 19th-century conditions of freedom for the haves and disenfranchisement of the have-nots. At the same time, amid the resurgence of open bigotry, the end of reform is stripping away illusions. It is reminding the people of Detroit and all of us, as Karl Polanyi identified in his classic text *The Great Transformation*, how the earth became commodified as land, how work became commodified as labor, how local economies were eclipsed by the power of global commerce and finance, and how democracy has always been a radical and dangerous concept.[4]

These are the profound terms of struggle that make our times rife with immense danger and boundless possibility. Historical sociologist Immanuel Wallerstein argues that the global capitalist system will not survive past 2050. Like the fluttering of butterfly wings that shape a hurricane thousands of miles away, small acts and breakthrough ideas will tilt our society toward a whole new social order that could be more democratic or authoritarian, participatory or exclusionary, egalitarian or plutocratic, sustainable or suicidal.[5] The fate of humanity rests on our capacity to think and act conscientiously.

ACKNOWLEDGMENTS

When I moved to Detroit 16 years ago, I never dreamed I would attempt to write a book about the city. That I developed the nerve to do so after starting from relative ignorance is a testament to the generosity of dozens of residents and activists who taught me to understand and love Detroit. I came to the city because of James and Grace Lee Boggs, whose visionary writing and organizing gave me a whole new sense of what it means to struggle for social transformation. While I never met Jimmy Boggs, I was blessed to have a close personal, intellectual, and political relationship with Grace through 17 life-changing years. Words cannot truly capture the immensity of my debt to her.

Sustained by an incredible grouping of board members and volunteers inspired by Jimmy and Grace, the Boggs Center to Nurture Community Leadership has been my movement home in Detroit and the world at large. My extended Detroit family draws from a wide array of community organizations, including Detroit Summer, Allied Media Projects, Detroit Asian Youth Project, and multiple groups and individuals named in the text. Among the many Detroiters who directly or indirectly supported my work on this book are adrienne maree brown, Wayne Curtis, Carl Edwards, Janice Fialka, dream hampton, Doc Holbrook, Shea Howell, Alice Jennings, Jenny Lee, Marcia Lee, Nate Mullen, Tawana Petty, Julia Putnam, Amanda

Rosman, Ron Scott, Yusef Shakur, Kim Sherobbi, Larry Sparks, Barbara Stachowski, Soh Suzuki, Myrtle Thompson-Curtis, and ill Weaver. Rich Feldman and Frank Joyce read and commented on a rough draft of the manuscript. D. Blair remains my spiritual guide to Motown.

This book would not be possible without the efforts of the wonderful staff at the University of California Press and several anonymous readers. I especially thank editors Lisa Duggan, Niels Hooper, and Curtis Marez for seeing its potential and helping it become a reality. I am honored to be included in the American Studies Now series amid many of our field's greatest beacons of light.

I deeply appreciate the School of Interdisciplinary Arts and Sciences and the University of Washington Bothell for providing my academic home, intellectual community, and material resources while I was writing. Wolf Yeigh, Susan Jeffords, Bruce Burgett, and Wayne Au provided invaluable administrative support. I often pinch myself when I think of how lucky I am to work among so many engaged scholars and critical thinkers, but while working on this book I particularly bounced ideas off Dan Berger.

I am humbled by the range of people and institutions across land and sea that invited me to share and discuss my work-in-progress: American Association of Geographers, American Studies Association, Chinese Progressive Association of San Francisco, Critical Ethnic Studies Association, Drexel University, Erasmus University College, Harvard University, Kalamazoo College, Michigan Equity Network, National Museum of American History, Organization of American Historians, Seattle University, Stanford University, University of Illinois–Chicago, University of Illinois–Urbana Champaign, University of Paris–Sorbonne, Vassar College, and Washington University.

For these formal opportunities and other, informal exchanges, I thank Matt Birkhold, Ned Blackhawk, Kevin Boyle, Lisa Brock, Evelyn Brooks Higginbotham, Amy Carroll, Jeff Chang, Joan May Cordova, Angela Davis, Tina Delisle, Andrew Diamond, Vince Diaz, Darren Dochuk, Ricardo Dominguez, Brian Doucet, Lauren Goodlad, Tom Guglielmo, Christina Hanhardt, Judith Howard, Walter Johnson, Robin D. G. Kelley, Audrey Kobayashi, Clarence Lang, Lisa Lee, David

Lloyd, Nicholas Mirzoeff, Nadine Naber, Konrad Ng, Amaka Oke-chukwu, David Palumbo-Liu, Jessi Quizar, Barbara Ransby, Fath Ruf-fins, Atef Said, Sarita See, Robert Self, Tyrone Simpson, Nico Slate, Maya Soetoro-Ng, Andrea Smith, Dean Spade, Lester Spence, Tom Sugrue, Alex Tom, Joe Trotter, Stephen Ward, and Deb Williamson. Michael Hardt deserves special mention for reading the complete manuscript and indulging me in several hours of conversation.

I am eternally grateful for the love and support of Mil and Nori Kurashige, Emily, Tula, Kori, and my family and friends in Los Angeles and Seattle.

This is a truncated list of those who helped guide me through many bumps in the road. To those I have omitted, please understand that my work always draws from collective thinking and action; I strive to give back as much as I can to the beloved community.

NOTES

ABBREVIATIONS

DETN   *Detroit News*
DFP   *Detroit Free Press*
NYT   *New York Times*

INTRODUCTION

1. Grace Lee Boggs, "In Detroit, We Have Just Begun to Fight," *Common Dreams*, August 18, 2013, http://www.commondreams.org /views/2013/08/18/detroit-we-have-just-begun-fight.

2. Data accessed from U.S. Census Bureau, http://www.census.gov.

3. Lani Guinier and Gerald Torres, *The Miner's Canary: Enlisting Race, Resisting Power, Transforming Democracy* (Cambridge, MA: Harvard University Press, 2003), 11–12.

4. Boggs, "In Detroit, We Have Just Begun to Fight."

5. For example, see Arlie Russell Hochschild, *Strangers in Their Own Land: Anger and Mourning on the American Right* (New York: The New Press, 2016); Katherine J. Cramer, *The Politics of Resentment: Rural Consciousness in Wisconsin and the Rise of Scott Walker* (Chicago: University of Chicago Press, 2016).

6. For an insightful overview of black politics and neoliberalism, see Lester Spence, *Knocking the Hustle: Against the Neoliberal Turn in Black Politics* (Brooklyn, NY: Punctum Books, 2015).

7. Ruth Wilson Gilmore, *Golden Gulag: Prisons, Surplus, Crisis, and Opposition in Globalizing California* (Berkeley: University of California Press, 2007), 26.

8. Rana Foroohar, "American Capitalism's Great Crisis," *Time,* May 12, 2016, http://time.com/4327419/american-capitalisms-great-crisis/.

9. Boggs, "In Detroit, We Have Just Begun to Fight."

10. Michael Hardt and Antonio Negri, *Multitude: War and Democracy in the Age of Empire* (New York: Penguin Press, 2004).

CHAPTER ONE. 1967

1. Martin Luther King Jr., "A Time to Break Silence," in *A Testament of Hope: The Essential Writings and Speeches of Martin Luther King, Jr.,* ed. James M. Washington (New York: HarperCollins, 1991), 231–244.

2. Ibid.; Martin Luther King Jr., "The Other America," March 14, 1968, http://www.gphistorical.org/mlk/mlkspeech/.

3. See Kevin Boyle, *Arc of Justice: A Saga of Race, Civil Rights, and Murder in the Jazz Age* (New York: Henry Holt, 2004).

4. Thomas J. Sugrue, *The Origins of the Urban Crisis: Race and Inequality in Postwar Detroit* (Princeton, NJ: Princeton University Press, 2005), 17–31, 91–123.

5. Sidney Fine, *Violence in the Model City: The Cavanagh Administration, Race Relations, and the Detroit Riot of 1967* (Ann Arbor: University of Michigan Press, 1989), 71–89.

6. George Galster, *Driving Detroit: The Quest for Respect in the Motor City* (Philadelphia: University of Pennsylvania Press, 2012), 155; Thomas Ford Hoult, "About Detroit ... We Told You So," *Crisis* 74 (October 1967): 407–410.

7. Fine, 96–120.

8. Ibid., 98–102, 122–123; Heather Ann Thompson, *Whose Detroit? Politics, Labor, and Race in a Modern American City* (Ithaca, NY: Cornell University Press, 2004), 38–43.

9. Transcript from *Bill Moyers Journal,* June 5, 2007, http://www.pbs.org/moyers/journal/06152007/watch3.html.

10. Fine, 155–156, 249–270, 299.

11. Ibid., 241, 383–391, quote on 353.

12. Ibid., 351, 370; Interview with Ed Vaughn by Sam Pollard, June 6, 1989, Henry Hampton Collection, Film and Media Archive, Washington University, St. Louis, Missouri, http://digital.wustl.edu/e/eii/eiiweb/vau5427.0309.166edvaughn.html.

13. Fine, 233, 299, quote on 300; *Report of the National Advisory Commission on Civil Disorders* (New York: Bantam, 1968), 105 (cited hereafter as "*Kerner Report*").

14. Fine, 193–202, 227–228, quote on 199.

15. Ibid., 241–270; *Kerner Report,* 107.

16. Fine, 271–290.

17. *Kerner Report,* 1, 10.

18. Ibid., 10–13.

19. Julian E. Zelizer, "Fifty Years Ago, the Government Said Black Lives Matter: The Radical Conclusions of the 1968 Kerner Report," *Boston Review,* May 5, 2016, https://bostonreview.net/us/julian-e-zelizer-kerner-report.

20. Fine, 371; Ahmad Rahman, "Marching Blind: The Rise and Fall of the Black Panther Party in Detroit," in *Liberated Territory: United Local Perspectives on the Black Panther Party,* ed. Yohuru Williams and Jama Lazerow (Durham: Duke University Press, 2008), 181–231.

21. Louis Lomax, "Organized Snipers in Riot Given Help by Residents," *DETN,* August 8, 1967.

22. Grace Lee Boggs, *Living for Change* (Minneapolis: University of Minnesota Press, 1998), 117–189.

23. Fine, 412–423; Rahman, 189.

24. Fine, 383–395.

25. Galster, 209–210; Thompson, 81–82, 99–100.

26. Elizabeth Hinton, *From the War on Poverty to the War on Crime: The Making of Mass Incarceration in America* (Cambridge, MA: Harvard University Press, 2016), 182–183.

27. *Kerner Report,* 18.

CHAPTER TWO. THE RISE OF THE
COUNTER-REVOLUTION

1. Bill McGraw, "Why Does L. Brooks Patterson Still Have a Coleman Young Problem?" *Deadline Detroit,* March 27, 2013, http://www.deadlinedetroit.com/articles/4270/why_does_l_brooks_patterson_still_have_a_coleman_young_problem. (McGraw notes that Young's speech was only 528 words.)

2. See Michel Foucault, *Society Must Be Defended* (New York: Picador, 2003).

3. Heather Ann Thompson, *Whose Detroit? Politics, Labor, and Race in a Modern American City* (Ithaca, NY: Cornell University Press, 2004), 197–204; Sidney Fine, *Violence in the Model City: The Cavanagh Administration, Race Relations, and the Detroit Riot of 1967* (Ann Arbor: University of Michigan Press, 1989), 457–458.

4. Interview with Ed Vaughn by Sam Pollard, June 6, 1989, Henry Hampton Collection, Film and Media Archive, Washington University, St. Louis, Missouri, http://digital.wustl.edu/e/eii/eiiweb/vau5427.0309.166edvaughn.html.

5. Lila Corwin Berman, *Metropolitan Jews: Politics, Race, and Religion in Postwar Detroit* (Chicago: University of Chicago Press, 2015), 1–17, 189–216.

6. Thomas J. Sugrue, *The Origins of the Urban Crisis: Race and Inequality in Postwar Detroit* (Princeton, NJ: Princeton University Press, 2005), 209–258; Joe T. Darden, Richard Child Hill, June M. Thomas, and Richard Thomas, *Detroit: Race and Uneven Development* (Philadelphia: Temple University Press, 1987), 138; Fine, 384.

7. Fine, 384, 436; Thompson, 206; Darden et al., 67; George Galster, *Driving Detroit: The Quest for Respect in the Motor City* (Philadelphia: University of Pennsylvania Press, 2012), 220–221.

8. Darden et al., 119–125; Sugrue, 76–77, 193.

9. Darden et al., 140–145; David Riddle, "HUD and the Open Housing Controversy of 1970 in Warren, Michigan," *Michigan Historical Review* (Fall 1998): 1–36.

10. Ze'ev Chafets, "The Tragedy of Detroit," *NYT,* July 29, 1990.

11. Kevin P. Phillips, *The Emerging Republican Majority* (New Rochelle, NY: Arlington House, 1969).

12. Samuel Sommers and Michael Norton, "White People Think Racism Is Getting Worse. Against White People," *Washington Post,* July 21, 2016; Pew Research Center, "On Views of Race and Inequality, Blacks and Whites Are Worlds Apart," June 27, 2016, 47.

13. Stanley B. Greenberg, *Middle Class Dreams: The Politics and Power of the New American Majority* (New Haven, CT: Yale University Press, 1996), 39.

14. Galster, 161–163.

15. L. Brooks Patterson, "Sprawl, Shmall. Give Me More Development," https://www.oakgov.com/exec/Pages/brooks/sprawl.aspx; Chafets, "The Tragedy of Detroit"; McGraw, "Why Does L. Brooks Patterson Still Have A Coleman Young Problem?"

16. Scott Kurashige, "Rereading Vincent Chin: Asian Americans and Multiracial Political Analysis," in *Minority Relations: Intergroup Conflict and Cooperation,* ed. Greg Robinson and Robert S. Chang (Jackson: University Press of Mississippi, 2017), 126–158.

17. Louis Aguilar, "Notorious Landlord Wants in on Downtown's Revival," *DETN,* August 31, 2006.

18. Joe T. Darden and Richard W. Thomas, *Detroit: Race Riots, Racial Conflicts, and Efforts to Bridge the Racial Divide* (East Lansing: Michigan State University Press, 2013), 54–66, 236–237; Suzette Hackney, "Suburban Cash, Detroit Drugs," *DFP,* May 8, 2003.

19. Michelle Alexander, *The New Jim Crow: Mass Incarceration in the Age of Colorblindness* (New York: The New Press, 2010), 6–12, 41–58; Dan Berger, *Captive Nation: Black Prison Organizing in the Civil Rights Era* (Chapel Hill: University of North Carolina Press, 2015), 269; Elizabeth Hinton, *From the War on Poverty to the War on Crime: The Making of Mass Incarceration in America* (Cambridge, MA: Harvard University Press, 2016), 5; Pew Center on the States, "One in 31: The Long Reach of American Corrections" (Washington, DC: Pew Charitable Trusts, 2009); Ruth Wilson Gilmore, *Golden Gulag: Prisons, Surplus, Crisis, and Opposition in Globalizing California* (Berkeley: University of California Press, 2007), 17.

20. Darden et al., 67; Galster, 220–221.

21. Darden et al., 27, 99, 255.

22. *Report of the National Advisory Commission on Civil Disorders* (New York: Bantam, 1968), 15; Nathan Bomey and John Gallagher, "How Detroit Went Broke," *DFP,* September 15, 2013.

23. Galster, 127–129; Bomey and Gallagher, "How Detroit Went Broke."

24. Chafets, "The Tragedy of Detroit."

25. Robert Reich, "The Political Roots of Widening Inequality," *American Prospect,* April 28, 2015, http://prospect.org/article/political-roots-widening-inequality; Galster, 124–127.

26. Elisabeth Malkin, "In Mexico, Automaking Is a Growth Industry," *NYT,* July 21, 2006; David Leonhardt, "$73 an Hour for Autoworkers and How It Really Adds Up," *NYT,* December 10, 2008; Thomas Bray, "Buyouts Reflect High Price of Detroit's Welfare Mentality," *DETN,* March 26, 2006.

27. Nick Bunkley, "U.A.W. Open to More Jobs at a Second-Tier Pay Level," *NYT,* March 30, 2011.

28. Mitt Romney, "Let Detroit Go Bankrupt," *NYT,* November 19, 2008.

29. Rana Foroohar, "American Capitalism's Great Crisis," *Time,* May 12, 2016, http://time.com/4327419/american-capitalisms-great-crisis/; Nomi Prins, *All the Presidents' Bankers: The Hidden Alliances That Drive American Power* (New York: Nation Books, 2014), 377–392.

30. Prins, 403–404.

31. Joel Kurth and Christine MacDonald, "Volume of Abandoned Homes 'Absolutely Terrifying,'" *DETN,* June 25, 2015; Melissa Maynard, "Michigan and Detroit: A Troubled Relationship," *USA Today,* July 31, 2013, http://www.usatoday.com/story/news/nation/2013/07/31/michigan-detroit-bankruptcy-bailout/2602505/; Steve Neavling, "Record Number of Detroit Police Live outside the City after 1999 Residency Law," *Motor City Muckraker,* January 3, 2017, http://motorcitymuckraker.com/2017/01/03/record-number-detroit-police-live-outside-city-1999-residency-law/; JC Reindl, "Home Values in Detroit Are Finally on the Rise," *DFP,* July 12, 2015.

32. *Adkins et al. v. Morgan Stanley et al., Class Action Complaint,* 12 Civ 7667 (2012).

33. Ibid.

34. Ibid.

35. John Gallagher, "Insider E-mails: Wall Street Pushed Bad Detroit Mortgage Loans," *DFP,* January 26, 2015, http://www.freep .com/story/money/business/michigan/2015/01/24/subprime-detroit-morgan-stanley/22286935/; U.S. Department of Justice, "Morgan Stanley Agrees to Pay $2.6 Billion Penalty in Connection with Its Sale of Residential Mortgage Backed Securities," February 11, 2016, https:// www.justice.gov/opa/pr/morgan-stanley-agrees-pay-26-billion-penalty-connection-its-sale-residential-mortgage-backed.

36. David Goldman, "CNNMoney.com's Bailout Tracker," *CNN. com,* http://money.cnn.com/news/storysupplement/economy/bailout-tracker/; Nathan Bomey, *Detroit Resurrected: To Bankruptcy and Back* (New York: W.W. Norton, 2016), 4–5.

37. Matt Helms, "Detroit Aims to Cut into Jobless Rate, Add Training" *DFP,* January 17, 2016; Council of Economic Advisers, "The Long-Term Decline in Prime-Age Male Labor Force Participation," June 2016.

CHAPTER THREE. THE SYSTEM IS BANKRUPT

1. Mark Maynard, "Everything You Ever Wanted to Know about the Emergency Manager Takeover of Michigan, and How We Allowed It to Happen," *MarkMaynard.com,* July 29, 2014, http://markmaynard .com/2014/07/everything-you-ever-wanted-to-know-about-the-emergency-manager-takeover-of-michigan-and-how-we-allowed-it-to-happen/.

2. *Stand Up for Democracy v. Secretary of State,* 492 Mich. 588 (2012).

3. "Michigan 2012 Election Results," *NYT,* http://elections.nytimes .com/2012/results/states/michigan; Evan Bonsall and Victor Agbafe, "Redrawing America: Why Gerrymandering Matters," *Harvard Political Review,* May 24, 2016, http://harvardpolitics.com/united-states/ redrawing-america-gerrymandering-matters/; Tom Perkins, "Once Again, Michigan Dems Receive More Votes in the State House, but Republicans Hold onto Power," *MetroTimes,* November 16, 2016.

4. Local Financial Stability and Control Act, Michigan Public Act 436 (2012); Chad Livengood, "Snyder Vetoes Gun Legislation," *DETN,* December 19, 2012.

5. Naomi Klein, *The Shock Doctrine: The Rise of Disaster Capitalism* (New York: Metropolitan Books, 2007).

6. Robert Reich, "The Political Roots of Widening Inequality," *American Prospect,* April 28, 2015, http://prospect.org/article/political-roots-widening-inequality.

7. David Harvey, "Neoliberalism as Creative Destruction," *Annals of the American Academy of Political and Social Science* 610 (March 2007): 30–31.

8. Ibid.

9. Nathan Bomey, *Detroit Resurrected: To Bankruptcy and Back* (New York: W.W. Norton, 2016), 13.

10. Nathan Bomey and John Gallagher, "How Detroit Went Broke," *DFP,* September 15, 2013.

11. Ibid.

12. Ibid.; Robert Snell and Chad Livengood, "Close Ties Put Detroit Pension Deal Brokers under Scrutiny," *DETN,* February 7, 2014; Darrell Preston and Chris Christoff, "Only Wall Street Wins in Detroit Crisis Reaping $474 Million Fee," *Bloomberg News,* March 13, 2013, http://www.bloomberg.com/news/2013–03–14/only-wall-street-wins-in-detroit-crisis-reaping-474-million-fee.html.

13. "Detroit Council: Four Members Push City Closer to Financial Brink," *DFP,* February 4, 2005; Marisol Bello, "Cops Told to Retrieve Council Members," *DFP,* January 22, 2005.

14. Kristin Longley, "Emergency Manager Michael Brown Appointed to Lead Flint through Second State Takeover," *MLive.com,* November 29, 2011, http://www.mlive.com/news/flint/index.ssf/2011/11/emergency_manager_michael_brow.html; Chris Lewis, "Does Michigan's Emergency-Manager Law Disenfranchise Black Citizens?" *The Atlantic,* May 9, 2013, http://www.theatlantic.com/politics/archive/2013/05/does-michigans-emergency-manager-law-disenfranchise-black-citizens/275639/.

15. Paul Egan, "After Court Threat, State Removed Flint's Power to Sue," *DFP,* September 19, 2016.

16. Adam Liptak, "Voting Rights Law Draws Skepticism from Justices," *NYT,* February 28, 2013; Charlotte Alter, "Detroit Voting Machine Failures Were Widespread on Election Day," *Time,* Decem-

ber 13, 2016, http://time.com/4599886/detroit-voting-machine-failures-were-widespread-on-election-day/.

17. Monica Davey and Mitch Smith, "2 Former Flint Emergency Managers Charged over Tainted Water," *NYT,* December 21, 2016.

18. George F. Will, "Detroit's Death by Democracy," *Washington Post,* August 1, 2013.

19. Andrew O'Hehir, "Why the Right Hates Detroit: How the Fates of Two Great Cities, Detroit and New Orleans, Symbolize What's Gone Wrong with America," *Salon,* July 27, 2013, http://www.salon.com/2013/07/27/why_the_right_hates_detroit/; Joanna Slater, "Detroit: A Lose-Lose Situation for All Involved," *The Globe and Mail,* July 19, 2013, http://www.theglobeandmail.com/news/world/a-lose-lose-situation-for-all-involved/article13330627/.

20. Paige Williams, "Drop Dead, Detroit!" *The New Yorker,* January 27, 2014, 32–39.

21. Detroiters Resisting Emergency Management, "People's Plan for Restructuring toward a Sustainable Detroit," February 24, 2014.

22. "Fourth Amended Disclosure Statement with Respect to Fourth Amended Plan for the Adjustment of Debts of the City of Detroit," May 5, 2014, *In re City of Detroit, Michigan,* U.S. Bankruptcy Court, Eastern District of Michigan, Southern Division, 116.

23. Ibid., 117.

24. Bomey, 51; "Orr Outlines Pension-Cut Plans for Detroit Workers," *Crain's Detroit Business,* June 21, 2013, http://www.crainsdetroit.com/article/20130621/NEWS01/130629980/orr-outlines-pension-cut-plans-for-detroit-workers; Matt Helms and Joe Guillen, "Even with City's Staggering Debt, Orr Says: Safety of Detroiters Is a Priority," *DFP,* June 11, 2013.

25. Bomey, 69.

26. Ibid., 79.

27. Ibid., 100.

28. "Tracking the Libor Scandal," *NYT,* March 23, 2016, http://www.nytimes.com/interactive/2015/04/23/business/dealbook/db-libor-timeline.html?; Cate Long, "Detroit's Embedded Time Bomb," *Reuters,* October 23, 2013, http://blogs.reuters.com/muniland/2013/10/23/detroits-

embedded-time-bomb/; Nomi Prins, *All the Presidents' Bankers: The Hidden Alliances That Drive American Power* (New York: Nation Books, 2014), 420.

29. Bomey, 100–165; Caitlin Devitt, "Leaving Bankruptcy, Detroit Takes on $1.28B of New Debt," *The Bond Buyer,* December 11, 2014, http://www.bondbuyer.com/news/regionalnews/leaving-bankruptcy-detroit-takes-on-1b-of-new-debt-1068692-1.html.

30. Bomey, 140–172, quote on 169.

31. Ibid., 158–159.

32. Ibid., 225–230.

33. "Fourth Amended Disclosure Statement," 157–158.

34. Bomey, 178, 232; Tresa Baldas and Christina Hall, "Rizzo Trash Empire Toppled," *DFP,* October 26, 2016; City of Detroit, "Ten-Year Plan of Adjustment Restructuring and Reinvestment Initiatives," Exhibit I of "Fourth Amended Disclosure Statement," 34.

35. Bomey, 232; "Ten-Year Plan of Adjustment," 65–57; Martin Lukacs, "Detroit's Water War: A Tap Shut-off That Could Impact 300,000 People," *The Guardian,* June 25, 2014, https://www.theguardian.com/environment/true-north/2014/jun/25/detroits-water-war-a-tap-shut-off-that-could-impact-300000-people.

36. Food and Water Europe, "Veolia Environment: A Profile of the World's Largest Water Service Corporation," April 2011; Bomey, 181–192.

37. Michigan Financial Review Commission Act, Michigan Public Act 181 (2014).

38. Kevyn D. Orr, "Final Report with Respect to the Financial Condition of the City of Detroit," December 9, 2014, http://www.michigan.gov/documents/treasury/Detroit_Final_EM_Report_476225_7.pdf; "Fourth Amended Disclosure Statement," 118–121, 161–162.

39. Danielle Ivory, Ben Protess, and Kitty Bennett, "When You Dial 911 and Wall Street Answers," *NYT,* June 26, 2016; Danielle Ivory, Ben Protess, and Griff Palmer, "In American Towns, Private Profits From Public Works," *NYT,* December 25, 2016.

40. "Fourth Amended Disclosure Statement," 162.

41. George Hunter, "Detroit Police Officials to Discuss Stop-and-Frisk," *DETN,* January 20, 2014; Gus Burns, "Police Chief Says Detroit Is Not a Sanctuary City," *MLive.com,* February 13, 2017, http://www.mlive.com/news/detroit/index.ssf/2017/02/police_chief_says_detroit_is_n.html.

CHAPTER FOUR. RACE TO THE BOTTOM

1. Darren A. Nichols and Christine Ferretti, "Detroit Official Is Suspended," *DETN,* October 11, 2013.

2. Brent Snavely, "Detroit's New CFO Ready to Get Tough," *DFP,* July 24, 2013; David M. Katz, "'Pit Bull' CFO Drives Detroit Turnaround," *CFO,* August 6, 2013, http://ww2.cfo.com/bankruptcy/2013/08/pit-bull-cfo-drives-detroit-turnaround/.

3. Nichols and Ferretti, "Detroit Official Is Suspended"; Christine Ferretti, "CFO Resigns amid Claims of Racial Comments," *DETN,* October 16, 2013.

4. Joe T. Darden, Richard Child Hill, June M. Thomas, and Richard Thomas, *Detroit: Race and Uneven Development* (Philadelphia: Temple University Press, 1987), 207; Keeanga-Yamahtta Taylor, *From #BlackLivesMatter to Black Liberation* (Chicago: Haymarket Books, 2016), 15, 79.

5. Nathan Bomey, *Detroit Resurrected: To Bankruptcy and Back* (New York: W.W. Norton, 2016), 34.

6. Daniel T. Moss to Kevyn Orr, January 31, 2013, https://www.scribd.com/document/155424185/Detroit-EM-emails; Jim Harger, "Kevyn Orr Thanks Outstate Legislators, Praises Gov. Rick Snyder, after Detroit Bankruptcy," *MLive.com,* January 26, 2015, http://www.mlive.com/business/west-michigan/index.ssf/2015/01/kevyn_orr_thanks_outstate_legi.html.

7. Christine Ferretti and Robert Snell, "City's Chapter 9 Fees Top $170M," *DETN,* December 31, 2014; "Meet Ken Buckfire," Paul and Daisy Soros Fellowships for New Americans, September 3, 2015, https://www.pdsoros.org/news-events/2015/09/03/meet-ken-buckfire; Robert Snell, "Talks on $140M in Ch. 9 Fees to Start," *DETN,* December 3, 2014.

8. Matt Helms, "Make Council Part-Time, Cut Its Staff, Report Recommends," *DFP,* April 9, 2013.

9. Jeff Wattrick, "22-Year-Old Consultant Billing Detroit Bankruptcy $275/Hour," *Deadline Detroit,* August 13, 2013, http://www.deadline detroit.com/articles/6012/22-year-old_consultant_billing_detroit_ bankruptcy_275_hour; "Conway Mackenzie Throws 25th Anniversary Bash in Detroit for $1.5 Million," *Huffington Post,* July 6, 2012, http://www .huffingtonpost.com/2012/07/06/conway-mackenzie-25th-anniversary-bash-15-million_n_1654659.html; Steve Neavling, "Ex-Treasurer Dillon Lands Job with Firm He Helped Get a Lucrative Contract in Detroit," *Motor City Muckraker,* February 19, 2014, http://motorcitymuckraker. com/2014/02/19/exclusive-ex-treasurer-dillon-lands-job-with-firm-he-helped-get-a-lucrative-contract-in-detroit/.

10. Ferretti and Snell, "City's Chapter 9 Fees Top $170M"; Joe Guillen, "Law Firm Slashed $17.7 Million from Detroit Bankruptcy Bills," *DFP,* January 17, 2015; Chad Livengood, "Rhodes Hired to Advise Puerto Rico on Debt," *DETN,* June 30, 2015; Claire Bushey, "Bankruptcy Fee Examiner," *Crain's Detroit Business,* November 24, 2014; "Who Got Paid in Detroit Bankruptcy Case," *DFP,* December 31, 2014.

11. Kellie Woodhouse, "Detroit Emergency Manager Kevyn Orr Described as 'Loyal Wolverine' and University of Michigan Law School Grad," *MLive.com,* March 17, 2013, http://www.annarbor .com/news/detroit-emergency-manager-kevyn-orr-described-a-loyal-wolverine-and-university-of-michigan-law-schoo/; "Miller Canfield Lawyers to Discuss Emergency Manager Laws at ABA State and Local Government Section Meeting," August 2, 2013, http://www .millercanfield.com/newsevents-news-1074.html.

12. Joel Kurth and Chad Livengood, "Records: EM Has Tax Liens on Home," *DETN,* March 16, 2013.

13. Bomey, 62.

14. Allysia Finley, "Kevyn Orr: How Detroit Can Rise Again," *Wall Street Journal,* August 2, 2013.

15. "Detroit Emergency Manager Kevyn Orr, '83, Speaks to Michigan Law Students," video recording, November 7, 2013, http://web.law .umich.edu/flashmedia/public/Default.aspx?mediaid = 3714.

16. Stephen Henderson, "Delinquent Loans Show Detroit Still Has a Ways to Go on Comeback Trail," *DFP,* May 12, 2013.

17. Joe Guillen, "Pension Funds' Saga May Be Ending," *DFP,* May 11, 2016.

18. Patricia Anstett, "$1.5 Billion for New DMC," *DFP,* March 20, 2010.

19. "Detroit Emergency Manager … Speaks to Michigan Law Students."

20. Eric Lacy, "Detroit Mayoral Candidate Mike Duggan Addresses Race Issues Openly," *Mlive.com,* February 11, 2013, http://www.mlive.com /detroit-river/index.ssf/2013/02/detroit_mayoral_candidate_mike.html; "Detroit Mayoral Candidate: Race Is Not an Issue," *BET.com,* August 8, 2013, http://www.bet.com/news/national/2013/08/08/detroit-mayoral-candidate-race-is-not-an-issue.html; Lisa M. Collins and David Josar, "Unlikely Voters Pick Kilpatrick," *DETN,* December 7, 2005; City of Detroit, "Official Results: Nov. 5, 2013 General Election," http:// www.detroitmi.gov/How-Do-I/Obtain-Voter-Information/Election-Results.

21. Allie Gross, "Duggan's Legacy Blighted by Questionable Rehab Projects," *MetroTimes,* July 20, 2016.

22. Karen Bouffard and Joel Kurth, "State Probes Dirty DMC Instruments," *DETN,* August 26, 2016.

23. Curt Guyette, "Onward Christian Scholars," *MetroTimes,* June 26, 1996; Katherine Stewart, "Betsy DeVos and God's Plan for Schools," *NYT,* December 13, 2016; Betsy DeVos, "Families Don't Need DPS Retread," *DETN,* February 22, 2016, http://www.detroitnews.com/story/opinion /2016/02/22/devos-families-need-dps-retread/80788340/.

24. Diane Bukowski, "Detroit Will Be Paying for School Bonds until Year 2040," *Voice of Detroit,* March 3, 2016, http://voiceofdetroit. net/2016/03/03/detroit-will-be-paying-for-school-bonds-until-year-2040-dismantling-of-dps-all-about-corporate-greed/; John Grover and Yvette van der Velde, "A School District in Crisis: Detroit's Public Schools, 1842–2015" (Loveland Technologies, n.d.), https://makelove-land.com/reports/schools; Chastity Pratt Dawsey, "Officials' Mistake Cancels Head Start in Detroit Schools," *Bridge Magazine,* June 10, 2014, http://bridgemi.com/2014/06/officials-mistake-cancels-head-start-in-

detroit-schools-sin-and-a-shame-for-district/; Alexandria Neason, "Held Back: Battling for the Fate of a School District," *Harper's*, October 2016, http://harpers.org/archive/2016/10/held-back/; Ann Zaniewski, "EAA to Pay $2.25 Million to Detroit District, Return Schools by July," *DFP*, November 7, 2016.

25. Grover and van der Velde, "A School District in Crisis."

26. Mark Binelli, *Detroit City Is the Place to Be: The Afterlife of an American Metropolis* (New York: Metropolitan Books, 2012), 120–124.

27. Natalie Matutschovsky, "Teen Moms in Detroit: Fighting to Save the School That Saved Them," *Time*, May 12, 2011, http://time.com/3777080/teen-moms-in-detroit-fighting-to-save-the-school-that-saved-them/.

28. Chastity Pratt Dawsey, "A Brief History of Proposal A, or How We Got Here," *Bridge Magazine*, April 29, 2014, http://www.bridgemi.com/talent-education/brief-history-proposal-or-how-we-got-here.

29. Grover and van der Velde, "A School District in Crisis."

30. Kate Zernike, "Heralded Choice Fails to Fix Detroit Schools," *NYT*, June 29, 2016; Nick Anderson, "Education Secretary Calls Hurricane Katrina Good for New Orleans Schools," *Washington Post*, January 30, 2010; Dave Murray, "Arne Duncan: Detroit Schools Are 'Ground Zero,' Changes Coming Soon," *MLive.com*, April 8, 2011, http://www.mlive.com/education/index.ssf/2011/04/arne_duncan_detroit_schools_ar.html.

31. Zernike, "Heralded Choice Fails to Fix Detroit Schools"; Jennifer Dixon, "Michigan Spends $1B on Charter Schools but Fails to Hold Them Accountable," *DFP*, August 24, 2016.

32. Zernike, "Heralded Choice Fails to Fix Detroit Schools."

33. Chastity Pratt Dawsey, "A *Bridge* Q-and-A with Detroit's Big 3 Education Chiefs," *Bridge Magazine*, March 31, 2016, http://bridgemi.com/2016/03/a-bridge-q-and-a-with-detroits-big-3-education-chiefs/; Erin Einhorn, "Why Detroit Is an Education-Funding Vacuum," *The Atlantic*, July 31, 2016, http://www.theatlantic.com/education/archive/2016/07/why-detroit-is-an-education-funding-vacuum/493589//; Ann Zaniewski, "EAA to Pay $2.25 Million to Detroit District," *DFP*, November 8, 2016.

34. Neason, "Held Back"; Jonathan Oosting and Shawn D. Lewis, "Snyder Signs $617 Million DPS Bailout Package," *DETN*, June 22, 2016;

Erin Einhorn, "Here's Which Detroit Schools Could Be Closed," *Chalkbeat,* September 28, 2016, http://www.chalkbeat.org/posts/detroit/2016/09/28/heres-which-detroit-schools-could-be-closed-as-confusion-about-their-future-deepens/.

35. Stephen Henderson, "Money for Something?" *DFP,* September 4, 2016.

CHAPER FIVE. GOVERNMENT
FOR THE 1 PERCENT

1. David Segal, "A Missionary's Quest to Remake Motor City," *NYT,* April 14, 2013, http://www.nytimes.com/2013/04/14/business/dan-gilberts-quest-to-remake-downtown-detroit.html. (The headline in the print version of the story was "Motor City Missionary.")

2. Jennifer Bain, "Comeback City: New Detroit Doesn't Need Pity," *Toronto Star,* September 10, 2016.

3. M.H. Miller, "Don't Call It a Comeback: Detroit's Post-Bankruptcy Crisis," *Art News,* September 15, 2016, http://www.artnews.com/2016/09/15/dont-call-it-a-comeback-detroits-post-bankruptcy-crisis/; Siobhan Gregory, "Detroit Is a Blank Slate: Metaphors in the Journalistic Discourse of Art and Entrepreneurship in the City of Detroit," *EPIC Proceedings* (October 2012): 217–233.

4. "FAQs," http://belleisle-freedomcity.com/faq.

5. Michael Jackman, "Detroit's White Racist Heritage ... in Letters," *MetroTimes,* August 17, 2016, http://www.metrotimes.com/Blogs/archives/2016/08/17/detroits-white-racist-heritage-in-letters.

6. "Fourth Amended Disclosure Statement with Respect to Fourth Amended Plan for the Adjustment of Debts of the City of Detroit," May 5, 2014, *In re City of Detroit, Michigan,* U.S. Bankruptcy Court, Eastern District of Michigan, Southern Division, 156; Dustin Walsh, "Belle Isle Traffic to Go High-Tech for Transport Conference," *Crain's Detroit Business,* April 14, 2014.

7. John Mogk, "Island Tax Haven? Not So Crazy," *Crain's Detroit Business,* January 20, 2013, http://www.crainsdetroit.com/article/20130120/NEWS/301209984/other-voices-island-tax-haven-not-so-crazy.

8. Joanna Cagan and Neil deMause, *Field of Schemes: How the Great Stadium Swindle Turns Public Money into Private Profit* (Monroe, ME:

Common Courage Press, 1998), 84–103; Joe T. Darden and Richard W. Thomas, *Detroit: Race Riots, Racial Conflicts, and Efforts to Bridge the Racial Divide* (East Lansing: Michigan State University Press, 2013), 125.

9. Louis Aguilar, "Apartments' Sales Will Oust Residents," *DETN*, April 23, 2013; Ryan Felton, "How Mike Ilitch Scored a New Red Wings Arena," *MetroTimes*, May 7, 2014; JC Reindl, "Q+A on Arena," *DFP*, July 22, 2014.

10. Felton, "How Mike Ilitch Scored"; Louis Aguilar and Christine Ferretti, "Fines Pile Up over Arena Workforce," *DETN*, October 12, 2016.

11. Felton, "How Mike Ilitch Scored"; Bill Bradley, "Dan Gilbert-Backed Bill Would Allow Developers to Pocket Even More Public Money," *Deadspin*, September 19, 2016, http://deadspin.com/dan-gilbert-backed-bill-would-allow-developers-to-pocke-1786813314.

12. "Shakin Street," *MetroTimes*, November 3, 2004.

13. Richard L. Florida, *The Rise of the Creative Class: And How It's Transforming Work, Leisure, Community and Everyday Life* (New York: Basic Books, 2002); Tracie McMillan, "Can Whole Foods Change the Way Poor People Eat?" *Slate*, November 19, 2014, http://www.slate.com/articles/life/food/2014/11/whole_foods_detroit_can_a_grocery_store_really_fight_elitism_racism_and.html; Joe Guillen and JC Reindl, "Former City Arena Negotiators Now Consult for Ilitches," *DFP*, February 13, 2016.

14. James Boggs, "Rebuilding Detroit: An Alternative to Casino Gambling," in *Pages from a Black Radical's Notebook: A James Boggs Reader*, ed. Stephen M. Ward (Detroit: Wayne State University Press, 2011), 345.

15. Stacy Perman, "The Real History of America's Most Authentic Fake Brand," *Inc.* (April 2016), http://www.inc.com/magazine/201604/stacy-perman/shinola-watch-history-manufacturing-heritage-brand.html.

16. Joe Nocera, "Is Motown Getting Its Groove Back?" *NYT*, June 2, 2015.

17. Louis Aguilar, "Putting a Price Tag on Gilbert-Related Holdings," *DETN*, April 29, 2016.

18. Josh Linkner, "Wish You Bought Gold in '06? You'll Wish You Bought Detroit in '12," *Forbes*, August 30, 2012, http://www.forbes.com

/sites/joshlinkner/2012/08/30/wish-you-bought-gold-in-06-youll-wish-you-bought-detroit-in-12/; Aguilar, "Putting a Price Tag on Gilbert-Related Holdings"; Corey Williams, "Whites Moving to Detroit, City That Epitomized White Flight," *U.S. News & World Report,* May 21, 2015,http://www.usnews.com/news/business/articles/2015/05/21/whites-moving-to-detroit-city-that-epitomized-white-flight.

19. Eric D. Lawrence, "1st Peek at New Streetcar," *DFP,* September 22, 2016.

20. Bill Laitner, "Heart and Sole: Detroiter Walks 21 Miles in Work Commute," *DFP,* February 1, 2015; 2000 U.S. Census data, https://factfinder.census.gov/.

21. Thomas J. Sugrue, "Notown," *Democracy* 28 (Spring 2013): 116–123; Nancy Kaffer, "Panopticon: Who's Watching the Watchmen?" *DFP,* March 22, 2015; Nancy Kaffer, "Watching Dan Gilbert's Watchmen," *DFP,* May 19, 2015; Steve Neavling, "Dan Gilbert's Surveillance Teams Messes *[sic]* with Wrong Detroit Institution," *Motor City Muckraker,* April 26, 2015, http://motorcitymuckraker.com/2015/04/26/dan-gilberts-surveillance-teams-messes-with-wrong-detroit-institution/; Nolan Finley, "Belle Isle Rowdies Shift Downtown," *DETN,* June 26, 2014.

22. Neavling, "Dan Gilbert's Surveillance"; Christine MacDonald and Joel Kurth, "Gilbert, Quicken Loans Entwined in Detroit Blight," *DETN,* July 1, 2015; Nolan Finley, "Quicken Loans' Dan Gilbert Sharpens Political Radar," *DETN,* June 29, 2016, http://www.detroitnews.com/story/opinion/columnists/nolan-finley/2016/06/29/quicken-loans-dan-gilbert-gets-political-sort/86540376/.

23. JC Reindl, "The Rising Cost of Living Downtown," *DFP,* December 7, 2014.

24. Bill McGraw, "Meet the Downtown Residents Who Say They Are Being Pushed Aside for the 'New Detroit,'" *Deadline Detroit,* May 2, 2013, http://www.deadlinedetroit.com/articles/4721/meet_the_downtown_residents_who_say_they_are_being_pushed_aside_for_the_new_detroit.

25. Eugene L. Birch, *Who Lives Downtown* (Washington, DC: Brookings Institution, 2005).

26. Christine MacDonald, "Aid Plans Ease Foreclosures, but Default Fears Shift to Taxes," *DETN,* September 8, 2016.

27. Ibid.; Todd Spangler, "Feds Give Michigan $188M More to Fight Blight," *DFP,* April 20, 2016; John Eligon, "Detroiters' Good Intentions Are Tested by Blight," *NYT,* December 13, 2014.

28. Mike Wilkinson, "City Dwellers Came for the Tax Breaks. Will They Stay When Breaks Expire?" *Bridge Magazine,* June 14, 2016, http://bridgemi.com/2016/06/city-dwellers-came-for-the-tax-breaks-will-they-stay-when-breaks-expire/; "Incentives," Live Downtown, http://www.detroitlivedowntown.org/incentives/.

29. John Gallagher, *Revolution Detroit: Strategies for Urban Reinvention* (Detroit: Wayne State University Press, 2013), 66–76.

30. "About," Detroit Eviction Defense, http://detroitevictiondefense.org.

31. "Detroit 2016: Linking Struggles for Racial and Economic Justice," Detroiters Resisting Emergency Management, http://www.d-rem.org/detroit-2016-linking-struggles-for-racial-and-economic-justice/.

CHAPTER SIX. FROM REBELLION TO REVOLUTION

1. Diane Bukowski, "Mass Shut-offs, Mass Incarceration at Mound Road Prison for Protesters," *Voice of Detroit,* May 28, 2014, http://voiceofdetroit.net/2014/05/28/mass-water-shut-offs-mass-incarceration-at-mound-road-prison-for-protesters/.

2. Ibid.; Bill Wylie-Kellerman, "The Detroit Water Struggle: A Story," *Critical Moment,* September 30, 2014, https://critical-moment.org/2014/09/30/the-detroit-water-struggle-a-story/.

3. Larry Gabriel, "When the City Turned Off Their Water, Detroit Residents and Groups Delivered Help," *YES! Magazine,* winter 2015; Martin Lukacs, "Detroit's Water War: A Tap Shut-off That Could Impact 300,000 People," *The Guardian,* June 25, 2014, https://www.theguardian.com/environment/true-north/2014/jun/25/detroits-water-war-a-tap-shut-off-that-could-impact-300000-people.

4. Grace Lee Boggs with Scott Kurashige, *The Next American Revolution: Sustainable Activism for the Twenty-First Century* (Berkeley: University of California Press, 2012), 173.

5. Marian Kramer, oral history, in *Detroit Lives,* ed. Robert H. Mast (Philadelphia: Temple University Press, 1994), 103; Marian Kramer, oral history, August 6, 2007, https://sites.google.com/a/umich.edu /motor-city-voices/work-showcase/kramer.

6. We the People of Detroit Community Research Collective, *Mapping the Water Crisis: The Dismantling of African American Neighborhoods in Detroit, Volume One* (Detroit: Author, 2016).

7. Valerie Vande Panne, "Life without Money in Detroit's Survival Economy," *Bloomberg,* January 12, 2017, https://www.bloomberg.com /news/features/2017–01–12/life-without-money-in-detroit-s-survival-economy.

8. Boggs with Kurashige, xxii; Elizabeth Royte, "What Lies Ahead for 3-D Printing?" *Smithsonian Magazine,* May 2013, http://www .smithsonianmag.com/science-nature/what-lies-ahead-for-3-d-printing-37498558/.

9. Matthew Piper, "Fab Lab and the Language of Nature," *Model D,* November 12, 2013, http://www.modeldmedia.com/features/greencity 1113.aspx.

10. Lori Higgins, "DPS Board Files Federal Lawsuit against State," *DFP,* April 8, 2016.

11. Jennifer Chambers, "Suit Says Detroit Kids Denied Right to Literacy," *DETN,* September 14, 2016; John Wisely, "State Says Reading Is Not a Right for Children," *DFP,* November 22, 2016.

12. Julia Putnam, "A Lifelong Search for Real Education," *YES! Magazine,* Fall 2009; University of Michigan data, http://ro.umich.edu/ enrollment/ethnicity.php.

13. Putnam, "A Lifelong Search."

14. Curt Guyette, "A School of Their Own," *MetroTimes,* July 9, 2013, http://www.metrotimes.com/detroit/a-school-of-their-own /Content?oid=2145961.

15. Julia Putnam, email to author, January 7, 2017.

16. Ibid.; Tom Gantert, "Detroit Public Schools' Collapse Preceded Charter School Expansion," *Capcon,* May 23, 2016, https://www.michigancapitolconfidential.com/22449.

17. Boggs with Kurashige, 105–134.

18. Joe Guillen, "$175M Tax Break Buys Detroiters Only 15 Jobs," *DFP,* March 14, 2014.

19. María Arquero de Alarcón and Larissa Larsen, "Mapping Delray: Understanding Changes in a Southwest Detroit Neighborhood," in *Mapping Detroit Land, Community, and Shaping a City,* ed. June Manning Thomas and Henco Bekkering (Detroit: Wayne State University Press, 2015), 115–142; Jim Lynch, "Marathon Neighbors Feel Neglected," *DETN,* December 1, 2014; Jim Morris and Chris Hamby, "In Marathon's Shadow," *MetroTimes,* October 31, 2012.

20. Jim Lynch, "Enbridge to Pay $177M in Oil Spill," *DETN,* July 21, 2016; Ian Austen, "From Canadian Oil, a Black Pile Rises in Detroit," *NYT,* May 18, 2013.

21. Matthew Dolan, "New Detroit Farm Plan Taking Root," *Wall Street Journal,* July 6, 2012, https://www.wsj.com/articles/SB10001424052702304898704577479090390757800; Leslie MacMillan, "Vast Land Deal Divides Detroit," *NYT,* December 10, 2012, http://green.blogs.nytimes.com/2012/12/10/vast-land-deal-divides-detroit/; Tommy Airey, "White Supremacy and Class Privilege in Detroit," *The Mennonite,* May 27, 2015, https://themennonite.org/feature/white-supremacy-and-class-privilege-in-detroit/.

22. "A New Harvest for Detroit," *The Atlantic,* May 27, 2010, http://www.theatlantic.com/projects/the-future-of-the-city/archive/2010/05/a-new-harvest-for-detroit/57308/; Eleanor Smith, "John Hantz," *The Atlantic,* November 2010, http://www.theatlantic.com/magazine/archive/2010/11/john-hantz/308277/; John Gallagher, "15,000 Saplings to Take Root in Detroit," *DFP,* May 17, 2014.

23. MacMillan, "Vast Land Deal Divides Detroit"; Airey, "White Supremacy and Class Privilege in Detroit."

24. Rosa Parks, *Quiet Strength* (Grand Rapids, MI: Zondervan, 1994); Joe T. Darden, Richard Child Hill, June M. Thomas, and Richard Thomas, *Detroit: Race and Uneven Development* (Philadelphia: Temple University Press, 1987), 183–186.

25. Sara Safransky, "Greening the Urban Frontier: Race, Property, and Resettlement in Detroit," *Geoforum* 56 (2014): 237–248.

26. *Detroit Future City: 2012 Detroit Strategic Framework Plan* (City of Detroit, 2013).

27. David Ashenfelter, "Benny Napoleon Isn't Telling the Truth about Why the Feds Cracked Down on His DPD," *Deadline Detroit,* July 29, 2013, http://www.deadlinedetroit.com/articles/5813/benny_napoleon_isn_t_telling_the_truth_about_why_the_feds_cracked_down_on_his_dpd; Tresa Baldas, "Detroit Police Oversight Finishes," *DFP,* April 1, 2016; Diane Bukowski, "Killer Cop on the Loose," *Michigan Citizen,* February 10, 2008.

28. Ashenfelter, "Benny Napoleon Isn't Telling the Truth"; Baldas, "Detroit Police Oversight Finishes."

29. *Grable v. Brown,* 2005 Mich. App. Lexis 3173; Diane Bukowski, "Serial Killer Kops?" *Michigan Citizen,* April 15, 2000; Jack Lessenberry, "Facing Down Deadly Force," *MetroTimes,* January 17, 2001.

30. Grace Lee Boggs, *Living for Change* (Minneapolis: University of Minnesota Press, 1998), 209–227; Ron Scott, *How to End Police Brutality* (Detroit: Detroit Coalition Against Police Brutality, 2015), 46.

31. *Color of Violence: The INCITE! Anthology,* ed. INCITE! Women of Color Against Violence (Cambridge, MA: South End Press, 2006).

32. Oralandar Brand-Williams, "Weekley Won't Be Retried in Death," *DETN,* January 29, 2015; George Hunter, "Cop in Aiyana Stanley-Jones Shooting Reinstated," *DETN,* April 18, 2015.

33. Sarah Stillman, "The Throwaways," *The New Yorker,* September 3, 2012; *Nelson v. City of Madison Heights et al.,* "Opinion and Order Denying Defendant's Motion for Summary Judgement," Document 122 (E.D. Mich. 2015).

34. Mary M. Chapman, "17-Year Sentence in Michigan Shooting," *NYT,* September 4, 2014.

35. Yusef Shakur, *My Soul Looks Back: Life after Incarceration* (Detroit: Urban Guerrilla, 2012), 76–77, 128.

36. Ibid., 187.

CONCLUSION

1. Nathan Bomey, *Detroit Resurrected: To Bankruptcy and Back* (New York: W.W. Norton, 2016), 13–14; Kenneth A. Buckfire, "From Detroit to Greece: Revitalizing an Economy," Foreign Policy Association, YouTube video, March 4, 2016, https://www.youtube.com/watch?v = XCsHBlTO8uk; "What Puerto Rico Can Learn From Detroit's Bankruptcy," *Bloomberg News* video, February 25, 2016, http://www.bloomberg.com/news/videos/2016–02–25/what-puerto-rico-can-learn-from-detroit-s-bankruptcy.

2. John Perkins, *Confessions of an Economic Hit Man* (San Francisco: Berrett-Koehler, 2004).

3. David Barboza, "Deaths Shake a Titan in China," *NYT,* May 27, 2010; Conner Forrest, "Chinese Factory Replaces 90% of Humans with Robots, Production Soars," *Tech Republic,* July 30, 2015, http://www.techrepublic.com/article/chinese-factory-replaces-90-of-humans-with-robots-production-soars/; Michael Schuman, "Is China Stealing Jobs? It May Be Losing Them, Instead," *NYT,* July 22, 2016, https://www.nytimes.com/2016/07/23/business/international/china-jobs-donald-trump.html.

4. Karl Polanyi, *The Great Transformation: The Political and Economic Origins of Our Time* (Boston: Beacon Press, 2001).

5. Immanuel Wallerstein, *Utopistics: Or, Historical Choices of the Twenty-First Century* (New York: The New Press, 1998).

GLOSSARY

COUNTER-REVOLUTION A political movement to undo revolutionary
  social changes. In this book, the term refers specifically to the
  right-wing mobilization in response to the demographic growth of
  nonwhite urban populations and the political empowerment of
  minority groups through civil rights advances. It also refers to the
  threat that the democratic foundations of the United States may be
  undermined by authoritarianism.

DEINDUSTRIALIZATION The decline in factory work and production
  amid the rise of automation, outsourcing, and the knowledge-based
  economy, beginning in the 1950s. Although a national phenomenon,
  it is especially associated with the economic dislocation that
  workers and communities have endured in the "Rust Belt" region
  of the Upper Midwest, which includes Michigan.

GENTRIFICATION The process of lower-income residents being
  displaced by upper-income residents and businesses catering to
  them. In urban communities, the term often carries racial
  implications and is used to criticize predominantly white yuppies
  or hipsters moving into neighborhoods that had been majority
  black and brown.

NEOLIBERALISM The political and economic pursuit of corporate
  power over the past five decades, through such measures as tax

cuts and free-trade agreements designed to weaken workers' rights and government regulation. In the United States, neoliberalism overturned the New Deal–era (from the 1930s to the '60s) expansion of middle-class employment and social welfare programs and initiated a new period marked by class polarization and the assertion of private property interests.

RADICAL Favoring deep change in existing beliefs, practices, and structures. In a popular sense, the word refers to extremism. However, in the context of activism and political history, radicalism is associated with left-wing movements for social justice and transformative change. Far-right-wing movements are known as *reactionary,* which refers to a desire to return to older ideas of social hierarchy.

KEY FIGURES

COMMUNITY ACTIVISTS

JAMES AND GRACE LEE BOGGS Black–Chinese American couple; pushed community organizers to make distinction between rebellion and revolution.

CHARITY HICKS Her call to "wage love" became rallying cry of activists under emergency management regime.

MARIAN KRAMER Welfare rights organizer; embodies lineage of civil rights and Black Power movement.

JULIA PUTNAM "Freedom schooling" educator; works to unleash potential in urban youth.

RON SCOTT Former Black Panther and longtime organizer against police brutality.

MALIK YAKINI D-Town Farm organizer; sees urban agriculture as key to black self-determination.

EMERGENCY MANAGEMENT REGIME

KENNETH BUCKFIRE Investment banker; developed financial strategy for Detroit bankruptcy.

MIKE DUGGAN First white mayor since 1974; elected while city was under emergency management.

KEVYN ORR Corporate lawyer from Jones Day firm; served as emergency manager during 2003–04.

STEVEN RHODES Federal judge for Detroit bankruptcy; subsequently appointed emergency manager of Detroit Public Schools.

RICK SNYDER Wealthy businessman and Republican governor of Michigan; elected in 2010 and appointed emergency managers in Detroit and Flint.

HISTORIC FIGURES

JEROME CAVANAGH Young white mayor of Detroit during 1960s; came to symbolize failure of racial integration and liberal reform.

ALBERT CLEAGE Fiery black nationalist preacher and prominent Black Power movement leader; founded Shrine of the Black Madonna.

ORVILLE HUBBARD Longtime mayor of Dearborn; epitomized overt white supremacy of suburbs.

OTTO KERNER Led presidential commission to study and recommend response to urban rebellions of 1960s.

KWAME KILPATRICK "Hip-hop" mayor of Detroit during first decade of 21st century; resigned under scandal and criminal indictment.

L. BROOKS PATTERSON · Longtime and still active political leader of Oakland County; exemplifies white suburban antipathy toward Detroit.

RONALD REAGAN His presidency in 1980s swung suburban whites away from Democratic Party to embrace conservative social policy.

COLEMAN A. YOUNG First black mayor of Detroit held office from 1974 to 1994; beloved by many in the city but viewed as having ruined the city by many suburban whites.

WEALTHY DEVELOPERS, PRIVATE INVESTORS, AND INFLUENCE PEDDLERS

BETSY DEVOS Right-wing billionaire; advocates for charter schools and vouchers.

DAN GILBERT Billionaire; has bought up much of Downtown Detroit as home base for his financial and real estate empire.

JOHN HANTZ Promotes urban farming as corporate, for-profit venture.

ILITCH FAMILY Owners of Detroit Tigers and Red Wings; have put entertainment at center of massive redevelopment projects.

SELECTED BIBLIOGRAPHY

Boggs, Grace Lee. *Living for Change*. Minneapolis: University of Minnesota Press, 1998.

Bomey, Nathan. *Detroit Resurrected: To Bankruptcy and Back*. New York: W.W. Norton, 2016.

Boyle, Kevin. *Arc of Justice: A Saga of Race, Civil Rights, and Murder in the Jazz Age*. New York: Henry Holt, 2004.

Darden, Joe T., Richard Child Hill, June M. Thomas, and Richard Thomas. *Detroit: Race and Uneven Development*. Philadelphia: Temple University Press, 1987.

Fine, Sidney. *Violence in the Model City: The Cavanagh Administration, Race Relations, and the Detroit Riot of 1967*. Ann Arbor: University of Michigan Press, 1989.

Georgakas, Dan, and Marvin Surkin. *Detroit, I Do Mind Dying: A Study in Urban Revolution*. Chicago: Haymarket Books, 2012.

Hinton, Elizabeth. *From the War on Poverty to the War on Crime: The Making of Mass Incarceration in America*. Cambridge, MA: Harvard University Press, 2016.

Spence, Lester. *Knocking the Hustle: Against the Neoliberal Turn in Black Politics*. Brooklyn, NY: Punctum Books, 2015.

Sugrue, Thomas J. *The Origins of the Urban Crisis: Race and Inequality in Postwar Detroit.* Princeton, NJ: Princeton University Press, 2005.

Thompson, Heather Ann. *Whose Detroit? Politics, Labor, and Race in a Modern American City.* Ithaca, NY: Cornell University Press, 2004.